ART OF
SUCCESSFUL
DEER HUNTING

OTHER BOOKS FROM WILLOW CREEK PRESS:

Stories of the Old Duck Hunter & Other Drivel
Bird Hunting Tactics
Complete Guide To Walleye Fishing
Secrets of a Muskie Guide
The Bucks Camp Log
European Recipes For American Fish & Game

ART OF SUCCESSFUL DEER HUNTING

Francis E. Sell

ART of SUCCESSFUL DEER HUNTING

Copyright © MCMLXIV by
Francis E. Sell
Published by
WILLOW CREEK PRESS
801 Oregon Street
Oshkosh, WI 54901

This is a 1980 edition of the hardbound book
published first as **The Deer Hunter's Guide**

Cover painting, "Last Glance — Whitetail", by Sharon Anderson,
courtesy of the artist and Willow Creek Gallery, 801 Oregon St.,
Oshkosh, WI 54901.

Price: $5.95
ISBN 0-932558-13-5
Printed in U.S.A.

Dedication

This book is respectfully dedicated to all the trappers, woods loafers and Indians with whom it has been my good fortune to hunt deer, to share camps, and listen to their talk about the "Hiyou skookum mowich."

Acknowledgments

I am deeply indebted to the editors of *Guns Magazine, Guns and Game, Gunsport, Gun and Hunting, American Rifleman,* and the *Archer's Magazine* for permission to use parts of this material which first appeared in these periodicals.

The trajectory tables are used with the kind permission of the Bausch and Lomb Optical Company.

All photographs were taken by the author; all deer were killed by the author—just to set the record straight.

Last, but not least, I am thankful for the distinct honor of having shared countless campfires with those truly fine deer hunters who find it impossible to stay indoors in autumn.

Contents

Foreword

The long shadows of an autumn evening are on the moist, misty slopes beyond my cabin as I write this. There is a trail leading away over the hills here, cut deep with deer tracks at its many turnings. Each autumn for more years than I like to remember, I have taken this trail, or one very similar, with deer hunting in mind.

Sometimes I hunted with a rifle. Sometimes my only excuse for being abroad in deer country was a camera. I hunted deer with a stopwatch, measuring the speed of their many gaits. With a portable range finder, I have measured the average distances at which they were killed. The inspiration for being abroad in deer territory in foul weather and fair, in spring, summer, autumn, and winter, has been the answer to a lifetime desire to learn all possible about deer, the most canny of all big game.

It has been my good fortune, over a lifetime of hunting, to have hunted with truly expert woodsmen, trappers, and Indians.

I have spent plenty of time hunting Columbia Blacktail, Mule Deer, and Whitetail Deer. The techniques of hunting have been essentially the same. True, in the more open Mule Deer territory, you widen the range and jump your deer at greater distances. But it takes the same guile and craft to outwit a Mule Deer as is required in successfully hunting the Whitetail Deer. You'll still hunt; you'll make drives; you'll trail watch—using all the techniques touched upon in this book.

These techniques have been successful in heavy cover and in open country. They have proved their worth on snow and on bare ground. I only ask that you measure them against the deer cover itself. They will determine the success of your hunt.

I am going deer hunting; you come, too.

FRANCIS E. SELL
Riverton, Oregon

Chapter 1

Deer
Rifle
Selection

DEER rifle selection is a major undertaking. There are many tangibles and intangibles to consider beyond actual caliber and ranging. A hunter must have a very acute knowledge of the average type shooting he'll be called upon to do in the multi-colored autumn forests.

To get this in focus, let's examine some of the actual elements of average deer shooting, on stand, driving, or still hunting in typical deer cover. The shot, as you probably know, will be taken at less than 100 yards, 50 yards being a long average. With the exception of the open range, long yardage shooting common in Mule Deer territory, specialized shooting in a few non-typical Whitetail and Columbia Blacktail sections, the targets will not be distant.

The chance of a shot will come with a built-in speed requirement which precludes any deliberate target-range stance or shooting technique. More to the point, this shot will be taken off-hand, and at a moving target. How fast this deer target is moving will be conditioned by the amount of skill brought into the still hunting, the driving or the deer stand occupancy.

If all this appears to complicate deer rifle selection, it is all to the good. Actually, one must get down to the basic considerations of deer rifle selection, much beyond the indicated casual consideration usually given the subject. Most choices of deer rifles are influenced too much by the prone target shot, the long-range small-game sniper—excellent segments of shooting sport. But when these narrow requirements of rifle desirability spill over into deer hunting, a practically unrelated sport, they are a decided handicap.

A rifle for average short-range deer shooting is compounded of three basic factors: *portability, speed in getting off the shot, and woods accuracy.* Deer rifle stocking fit is, of course, a personal matter. But it must be tied with the type of shooting expected. Best is a custom stock, of course. In this connection I recall readying a rifle for deer hunting, making the stock and testing for a perfect fit. During the entire routine I never once measured any of the usual stock dimensions, save the stock length, which I made 13½ inches. With a downward pitch of 2¼ inches, measured from the line of iron sights.

Bringing the rifle in for an *exact* fit for off-hand shooting, I worked the stock down between sessions of snapping it to my shoulder and aiming at deer in the apple orchard about my cabin. When I arrived at a fit which made it harder to not look through those sights once the rifle was at shoulder than to look through them at my selected and unsuspecting targets, I measured the dimensions.

Here is what I had all along the line: Drop at comb 1 9/16, level Monte Carlo. Drop at heel 2½ inches. The cheek piece is slightly concave to give full support, and to make sure the face comes to the exact contact for each shot.

These particular dimensions are not greatly different than those required for an upland shotgun, where most of the shots are taken at low flying birds. The personal factor, as previously pointed out, however, must be considered. Where one buys a ready stocked factory rifle, there is sufficient wood for the individual modifications which a deer hunter should make. These can be achieved with nothing more in the way of tools than a wood rasp and several grades of sandpaper. Best method, as indicated, is to *cut and try.* Snapping the rifle to the shoulder between sessions, reworking, until the sights come on target with no conscious effort, and with dispatch.

Accuracy in a deer rifle must be measured, not only by the size of the group it is capable of producing, but by the time element

12

required in getting off two or three shots. Accuracy is also a factor of gunner personality, tied in with rifle action.

If this last factor sounds esoteric, bear with me a moment and later I'll detail this very essential requirement. Another factor of accuracy which must not be overlooked is rifle weight. This is perhaps the least understood segment of the entire accuracy requirement. All too many hunters associate deer rifle accuracy with heavy weight—the heavier the rifle the more accurate. This concept, carried over from the target range, has no basis in fact. When a rifleman has a fast moving deer target before him, his time in which to make a killing shot is limited.

A deer rifle, of course, may be too light for best possible field shooting accuracy, but the usual inaccuracy stems from the opposite, overweight. Weight, proper weight, in a deer rifle is an intangible which is hard to reduce to pounds and ounces, except as it is measured in terms of gunning utility. If a hunter isn't conscious of either weight or whispy lightness in his deer rifle, he approaches the ideal heft and balance.

Such a deer rifle will feel no heavier, nor lighter, than one's arm in use. Indeed, it should feel as an extension and refinement of the individual's pointing ability—as natural as pointing with an extended arm and forefinger. This rifle weight, for the average hunter, will fall between 6½ and 7½ pounds for a fully equipped gun. Above this rifle weight, a hunter is conscious of sighting alignment. There is a feeling of deadly inertia. Below this weight there is a feeling of something lacking, like erratic snap and swing, or a lack of rhythm in gun mounting or pointing.

This type rifle weight makes a direct contribution to off-hand deer shooting accuracy, something which has only casual reference to making minute of angle groups for ten successive shots. In reality, a rifle which is incapable of making less than 3-inch groups at 100 yards, may, from the standpoint of clean killing, be more accurate than the nail-driving-precision gun which nips into the same ragged hole at the same yardage. For in the very nature of things, a deer hunter must give up a bit of target accuracy to gain maximum woods accuracy in his deer rifle.

Rifle balance and weight go hand in hand. Bring your rifle up for the shot at a fast moving target. Proper balance and weight does two things: it steadies you for the shot by automatically taking care of the *basic rifle alignment,* and it gives you a fast handling gun with which to take full advantage of the limited time element you have for making the shot.

My classic example of incorrect gun weight occurred when hunting with a very experienced woodsman, a man who dreamed deer and deer rifles during the closed season and one who was always refining his equipment in one direction or another. This particular day he carried a Savage, model 99, lever action—an excellent selection for deer hunting. During the off season he had a tang safety installed, sliding shotgun type, a very needed improvement. In addition, he had stoned the trigger pull to a crisp 3½ pounds. Stocking had been attended to by adjusting the factory stock to a more custom fit. All this, mind you, stemmed directly from years of experience, and these years certainly did improve the woods accuracy of the rifle—if he had stopped at this point.

But, beyond this, he decided to do something about the weight of his rifle which checked in at 7¼ pounds, 22-inch barrel, 300 Savage caliber. He had a gunsmith turn the barrel down. He worked the forearm over to remove a few additional ounces. He hollowed out the stock. Finished, his rifle weighed just short of 6 pounds, trailside.

The morning I have in mind, he was especially pleased with the portability of his rifle. He snapped it on a few marks as we left my cabin for the woods. No more seven pound rifles for him, no Sir.

We entered the woods, separated by an interval of about 80 yards, and worked our way through a broken hill country, pacing each other. We moved snail slow through the heavy cover, and there were plenty of fresh deer signs to keep us on our toes.

One phase of this still hunt took both of us into a steep canyon, then up the slope of a heavily wooded hill, working our way against the morning thermal set of the wind. Sure, we took it easy, knowing that any step in deer hunting worth taking should be taken cautiously, as if the entire hunt depended on the next move—as it often does.

Despite this cautiously slow going, we topped out on the heavily wooded ridge well winded. I looked to my left and could see the scarlet hunting jacket of my light-weight rifle friend. And, even as I caught the brilliant color of his jacket through the autumn woods, I heard his shots crash out against the morning stillness.

One, two, three. Then I heard some earnest cursing. After a short interval, I walked down ridge toward the disturbance which had now subsided into some mumblings and self incriminating growlings.

When I arrived, my scarlet-coated hunting friend was sitting on a log regarding his smartly tailored rifle. "Just missed the biggest buck I have seen during the past five years," he said. "Couldn't hold on him with this light contraption, not after coming up winded out of that brushy canyon."

I nodded my agreement. For I, too, had essentially walked the same trail one time, making up a light rifle—too light—and finding its short comings the hard way: with a big buck before me. Mine, however, was a light, 20-inch barreled .30/30, model 54. It, like his Savage, had all the emphasis on portability. In the clutch, and again like his customized Savage, it proved to be very inaccurate—as much so as if I had used a heavy target rifle for the touch and go of deer shooting.

Next week, hunting again with this same experienced outdoorsman, I noticed that his featherweight rifle had been cashiered. He now carried another Savage lever action—the stock customized for a more personal fit. The shotgun-type tang safety had been transferred from the light-weight rifle to this welter-weight. Within two days he had woods business again, downing a beautiful four pointer to fill his license. The shooting was much like that presented by the big buck which he had missed with the light-weight rifle.

Rifle weight is one factor pertaining to individual fit. There are others. A deer hunter is confronted with four different type actions from which to choose in selecting a suitable rifle. Most hunters give too little thought to the personal matching of proper rifle action to hunter temperament. Some deer hunters need the stabilizing influence of a good bolt action to steady them during the excitement of deer shooting. Other hunters, of more phlegmatic temperament, often need rifle action which doesn't require the deliberation of a bolt gun for a second shot. Quite often he cannot do his best rifle shooting with a fast, dynamic lever action. For him, the best selection is an auto-loader, or a pump action.

The worst possible combination is an auto-loader in the hands of a nervous, quick-triggered deer hunter. You seldom have to

The answer to the hunter's dreams.

prowl the autumn woods for any length of time to hear this type of hunter go through his skittish rifle routine. Four or five shots will rip out against the stillness of the woods, shots so closely spaced you know that gun pointing has been totally subordinated to speed of fire. Such hunters know they have a magazine full of cartridges, and all they have to do to blast off is pull the triggers of their auto-loaders—and that they do, with ineffective results. The steadying influence of a good, smooth operating bolt action would make a direct and accurate contribution to their shooting by steadying them at the critical moment when they jump game.

Only the individual hunter can know beyond the least rifle-shooting doubt which action will make the greater contribution to his rifle shooting. And he should give this very personal problem plenty of consideration, matching his temperament carefully to the rifle action, just as carefully as he matches rifle weight and stocking to his requirements.

The most important shot presented in deer hunting is the first one, for usually this is made at a slower moving, often unalarmed target. More, it is usually delivered when the rifleman has the best opportunity for a telling hit. Here, the deer hunter must consider the many options offered by the various safeties and hammers on the different type guns. For the basic factor of getting into action smoothly, taking full advantage of the limited time element inherent in all deer shooting, is, to a great extent, tied in directly with a hunter's ability to swiftly ready his rifle for that all important first shot.

Even if the shot is at a non-moving target, there is always the threat of immediate movement. If you are using a bolt-action rifle, look to the safety. Some are so slow that they can lose you the best of the time element presented for the shot. The shotgun-type sliding safety, such as is provided on the Husqvarna and other bolt-action rifles is best. This same shotgun-type, sliding tang safety is also good on the Savage, model 99—actually comes as standard equipment on one model.

The outside hammer of the model 94 Winchester, the model 71, and the Marlin Model 336 exemplifies the best in speed of the first shot among lever actions. This particular feature, on all the classic deer rifles, such as the famous .30/30 Winchester and

Marlin, is one of the reasons for their continued popularity among hunters.

When a shotgun-type safety is used, or the above mentioned outside hammer, readying for the first shot is always subconscious. Snap such an equipped deer rifle to the shoulder and it has the safety off as part of the mounting routine.

You can, of course, learn to use a trigger-type safety with fair speed; but employment for the trigger finger should be confined to triggering the shot, nothing else. The safety release, for best, most efficient, off-hand shooting, should be employment by the thumb alone.

Barrel lengths are of top concern for a hunter selecting a deer rifle. There has been a noticeable shortening of barrels in hunting rifles over the past decade, something which is all to the good. In bolt actions, to keep within a weight limit of not more than 7½ pounds, a 20- to 22-inch barrel length is about right. This makes for a highly portable gun, and it handles with top dynamic efficiency for the usual off-hand shooting.

A barrel length of 20 inches in a bolt-action rifle gives an over-all length of 40½ inches. Compare this with a length of 42½ inches for a lever action with a 24-inch barrel, such as the Model 71 Winchester, or the Marlin 336. Here, however, two inches lopped off the barrels of either the Model 71 Winchester, now obsolete, or the Marlin Model 336 make for faster handling deer rifles. In the case of the Model 71, with its weight of around 8 pounds, the removal of 2 inches from the barrel, along with a hollowing out of the stock, is required to bring it within the *best* weight limits for a deer rifle. This done, the Model 71 is one of the smoothest lever actions ever produced.

In going to a 20-inch barrel in the bolt action, I feel this length has a more finished appearance when it is complemented with a Mannlicher-type stock—full length forearm. This adds but a fraction of an ounce to the over-all weight, and the entire rifle appears more finished in every respect. A bolt-action rifle with a 20-inch barrel, stocked with a short forearm, appears dubbed off—more in a class with a sawed off shotgun.

A 20-inch barrel in any of the lever actions, however, is an excellent choice for average-range deer shooting. These can be had in Savage, Marlin, and Winchester. The Model 94 Winchester Carbine, and the Marlin version of this rifle, both with 20-inch barrels, still are the most popular of all deer rifles.

Trigger pulls are very important in readying a rifle for deer hunting. Fortunately, this long neglected item has been getting more attention of late from both the manufacturer and gunsmith. The improved version of the Savage, Model 99 now carries an excellent trigger pull. Those found on the Remington bolt actions are usually good, and fully capable of being adjusted. This is also true of the Winchester, Model 70, and the several versions of the Model 98 Mauser.

The essential requirement is a short crisp pull of not less than 3 to 3½ pounds. This pull should break like a winter icicle. There is no need for a lighter pull, and a heavier trigger pull than this is disturbing.

Most of the present auto-loaders have very heavy, creepy pulls. These pulls are quite heavy of necessity, but they certainly are not the best trigger pulls by any yardstick of field-shooting measurement. Within the outlined limits of 3 to 3½ pounds, trigger pulls are used without thought of their weight. A point is reached when the rifleman, with a little practice, seemingly wills the shot. He isn't conscious of applying the 3 to 3½ pounds required for the let-off. And this is a vital requirement for the touch and go of average deer shooting.

Last requirement of a deer rifle is a light carrying sling. You'll not use it as a target shot would, to steady your aim. On occasion, you'll sling your gun to your shoulder as you examine cover with your binoculars.

Just one other requirement must be noted here, the understudy rifle. This should be of the same weight, or close to the same weight as your deer rifle, but of a smaller caliber—quite often a .22 rim fire. It should have the same trigger pull and the same sights. In short, it is a substitute for your more powerful caliber, affording a means of cheaper rifle shooting practice.

This understudy rifle can be used at targets. It can quite often be used for off-hand pest shooting, with the thought that such practice will be invaluable, come autumn when you are prowling the deer covers. Fortunately, there are good understudy rifles available with all types of actions. So there is no excuse for less than a complete matching all along the line. It is for the hunter who is determined to become an expert deer-rifle shot.

19—Deer Rifle Selection

Chapter 2

Deer Rifle Bullet Deflection In Brush

SOMEHOW, with all the advances made in rifle velocities, with trajectory cut to a minimum, the brush-bucking deer hunter has been overlooked. He must, if he isn't acutely aware of the problem of bullet deflection in heavy cover, go to his deer hunting with something other than the best bullet weight driven at something other than the best velocity level. Indeed, if he is not too experienced, he may question the very real ballistic problem of erratic bullet performance in heavy cover, believing such reports of deflection to be old woodsmen's tales by hunters still in the black-powder days of velocities, bullet weight, and even caliber.

But the problem of bullet deflection in brush, you may bet your best hunting knife, is very real. Bullets, even the best, most modern ones, deflect at certain velocities to the point where they wound deer at short 45- to 50-yard shooting. The kindred problem of bullet blowup is almost equally bad, too. The best bullet weights, driven at proper heavy-cover velocity, turn in a top drawer performance. Such bullets have much in common, reducing *all* deer rifle calibers to a very common ballistic denominator.

Once still hunting a dense section of territory in my *Happy Hunting Grounds,* the hideout of a beautiful five-point buck, I had this soundly brought to mind. This buck occupied a jumble of broken brushy hills. The entire area was covered with a screening

20

of black huckleberry, vine maple, low spreading hemlock, and small spruce. A shot here, as I well knew, would be touch and go with no time to wait around for the game to clear the cover to any great extent, giving a totally unobstructed chance.

I roused this deer at a nominal 45-yard wood's range. He came smoking out of his bed, a silver shower of morning dew shaking from the huckleberry brush marking his course of direction. I got the shot the third time he hit the ground, taking it through a screening of huckleberry. At the rifle report I saw a vine maple limb fall slowly then hang by its partly severed base near its parent tree. My bullet had cut through it before entering the huckleberry brush.

I walked forward, rifle at the ready, half believing I had missed my buck in the heavy cover. But he was dead enough, with a bullet hole which entered just back of the near front leg and emerged in front of the off front leg. Bullet and caliber? I'll come to that directly.

After the shot, I tried to line up on my bullet deflection by going back to my shooting point, but it was a fruitless task. The twigs touched by the bullet in passage seemed well in line. And the target lay fifteen feet beyond the indicated bullet disturbance. I did know, beyond the least cavil of hunting doubt, that I had gotten excellent brush bullet performance, with no bullet deflection and no bullet blowup, the two requisites for successful shooting in heavy cover. I wondered, however, surveying the screening of brush through which my bullet had passed to reach the vital area on this buck, how many modern calibers recommended for deer hunting could have turned in the same high-grade performance? This question became the inspiration for a lot of bullet and velocity testing to find the *best* performance weight in bullets, the *best* velocity level for brush shooting.

Literally thousands of loads were tested, for just about all modern calibers and all bullet weights and velocities. I even spent time testing the old .45/70 with a 500-grain bullet driven at a velocity of 1,450 feet a second. The other extreme found me testing a 70 grain bullet at 3,500 feet a second. This testing turned up some very worthwhile data of a type which answers a lot of questions about why so many deer are left in the woods each autumn, wounded and unrecovered.

I used the standard NRA 100-yard, small-bore rifle targets, placing them at woods ranges of 45 yards. Between the firing point and target I had typical screening of brush, the type through which a deer hunter is often under the compelling necessity of angling a bullet for a clean kill.

After arranging my targets, I tested with several different calibers, several bullet weights and velocities. I checked for both deflection and bullet blowup. Obviously, all rifles remotely suitable for deer hunting couldn't be tested, but their bullet weights and velocities could be duplicated in other calibers. I used a .257 caliber with 100-grain bullet driven at a velocity of 2,900 feet a second. This could pinpoint the .250/3,000 Savage's ability as a brush bucker, the 6.5mm with 100-grain bullet at this velocity bracket or higher. It could serve for several of the wildcats in this caliber. It was with this caliber I started the series of tests.

Shooting at 45 yards, I got deflections of 7 and 8 inches with two shots. Both these bullets cut half-inch twigs four feet in front of the target. A second try, firing two more rounds, thick brush two feet before the target almost obscuring it, one bullet keyholed and struck about 4 inches from point of aim. The other bullet mushroomed before striking the target. It showed a deflection of 5 inches. Both these shots would have wounded a deer under the circumstances.

I fired two shots to the group, sometimes three, as this is the usual number a deer hunter gets in heavy cover. I wasn't interested in 10-shot target groups, which are totally unrealistic in this type testing.

Turning to the .243 Winchester, same 45 yards range, I tested a 100-grain bullet at a velocity of 3,000 feet a second. With the first two shots I got complete bullet blowup, the target behind a screening of huckleberry brush. Moving the target so the intervening brush consisted of vine maple and hazel, ranging in diameters from one-half to three-quarters of an inch, both bullets fired mushroomed before hitting the target. Deflection was 4½ inches with one, 6 inches with the other.

These bullets had dissipated their energy on the intervening brush to the point that a deer in the target area would have only been wounded. Unless the deer offered a neck shot, or stood so only the thin rib cage was point of aim, there would have been insufficient penetration with either of these bullets. Then, of course, with enough deflection to have only touched the fringe area of the essential target, classifying the .243 Winchester as an undesirable short-range deer rifle in heavy cover.

To examine comparatively high velocity bullet performance, the next rifle tested was a .228 Ackley Magnum Wildcat. This rifle was used with the Ackley Controlled Expansion Bullet, driven at a velocity of 3,500 feet a second. It had a weight of 70 grains. The .228 Ackley has proven to be a very good deer rifle in more open ranges, out to around 250 yards or so. But here, with ranges close to average woods distances of 45 yards, brush obscuring the target, results had little in common with the more open ranges.

First bullet blew up in front of the target, carrying through to hit point-of-aim with two large fragments. Second bullet showed deflection of 4 inches from point-of-aim. It expanded before reaching the target, and printed a 55-caliber hole. The third bullet key-holed, deflecting 5 inches from point-of-aim, all this with the target behind a screening of small alder and hazel.

With the target behind a screening of huckleberry brush I repeated this test. Both bullets keyholed. Both deflected 4 inches from point-of-aim. Here was no uniform brush bucking. Obviously, a deer hunter would be poorly armed with any rifle pushing a 70-grain bullet at 3,500 feet a second, average woods ranges.

Turning to the .270 Winchester and using a 130-grain bullet at a velocity of 3,140 feet a second, I failed to get any bullets on the paper target back of the alder and hazel thickets. With the target placed behind a light huckleberry screening, two out of three bullets touched the target. Both hits showed complete blowup.

The .270 Winchester caliber, using a 150-grain bullet at 2,800 feet a second, gave 5, 7, 3 inches of deflection from point-of-aim. A light screening of huckleberry brush was used. With the heavier alder and hazel brush obscuring the target, I got deflections of 8, 9, 6 inches. But in no case did the bullet show signs of tipping or blowup. When the 150-grain .270 caliber bullet was used at a reduced velocity of 2,600 feet a second, deflection showed 1½, 3, and 4 inches from point-of-aim in the heavy screening of alder and hazel. With the target placed behind a light screening of huckleberry brush, all shots fired printed on point-of-aim, showing no deflection or mushrooming before reaching the target.

A light handy combination for brush shooting—short 20-inch barreled, Mannlicher-stocked, 6.5x55mm rifle, using a 150-grain bullet and 2X scope

Turning to the .280 Remington, with a 100-grain bullet at 3,570 feet a second, I got no data at the target. In both types of brush screening, I got complete bullet blowup. Upping the bullet weight in this caliber to 165 grains, at a velocity of 2,800 feet a second, results were better, with deflections of 6, 5, 4, with the target placed behind a screening of huckleberry brush. With the heavy alder and hazel screening, deflection was 7, 6, 5 inches. When the velocity of this bullet was reduced to 2,500 feet a second, there was no measurable deflection with either type of brush screening.

I made no runs with any of the ultra-high velocity rifles. For the case against high velocity deer rifles in heavy cover was sufficiently proved with the .270 Winchester, the .280 Remington, and the .228 Ackley.

Turning to the .30/06, and using a 150-grain bullet at 2,900 feet a second, I got duplicates of the .270 and .280 performances with bullets in this velocity bracket and weight. But loading the 150-grain, .30/06 bullet down to a velocity of 2,500 feet a second, deflection in the heavier screening of alder and hazel measured out to 2, 3, 3½ inches. With the target behind a light screening of huckleberry brush, there was no measurable deflection.

Upping the .30/06 bullet weight to 180-grain, but retaining the same velocity of 2,500 feet a second, deflection was no problem.

Turning to the .35 Remington caliber, and using a 200-grain bullet at a velocity of 2,200 feet a second, I got deflection of 5, 3, and 2½ inches with the target behind a screening of hazel and alder. One bullet showed slight tipping. One bullet showed insipid expansion. In the light huckleberry brush screening, none of three shots showed any measurable amount of deflection from point-of-aim.

Using this same bullet weight in a .358 Winchester, at a velocity of 2,530 feet a second, the three shots through the alder-hazel screening printed a ⅞-inch group at point-of-aim. Moving the same target behind a light screening of huckleberry brush, three more shots printed into the same group, enlarging it to 1½ inches.

Two groups were fired with the 170-grain, .30/30 Winchester soft-point bullet, at a velocity of 2,200 feet a second. This old reliable deer caliber proved very good. The three shots fired at the target, a screening of huckleberry brush obscuring it, gave no measurable deflection. Moving the target behind the heavier brush, alder and hazel, I got deflection of only 1, 1½, and 3 inches. Obviously, the continued popularity of the .30/30, 170-grain loading has basis in solid ballistic fact.

To check the indicated *best* velocity level, I fired three shots at this point with a .45/70, 500-grain bullet. The velocity was a modest 1,450 feet a second. First test was with the target behind a heavy screening of alder and hazel. Two shots were fired. Both bullets went screaming off through the forest, wailing like Banshees. They deflected badly. Two more fired with the target behind a screening of huckleberry brush showed no measurable deflection.

One other deer rifle received my attention. I tested it to see if there was any great virtue in extra sectional density, or whether the best velocity level was tied in with bullet weight alone. This rifle, a 6.5X 55mm caliber, pushed a 156-grain bullet at 2,450 feet a second. I got no measurable deflection in either the heavy screening of brush, or the light. Velocity, it appeared, was of more importance than sectional density in a deer bullet for short-range shooting in heavy cover. This, I think, is further indicated by the caliber and bullet weight with which I took the buck mentioned in the first part of this chapter on brush bullets for deer.

My buck fell to a Model 71, .348 Winchester, pushing a 200-grain bullet at a velocity of 2,500 feet a second. The sectional density of this bullet figures out at a modest .258. This .348 loading has the same bullet weight and velocity level as a .358 Winchester.

Now we come to the basic question which all this testing poses: what calibers and bullet weights would have turned in a top drawer performance under the same circumstances as those I had when I took this buck?

First, a velocity level of between 2,200 and 2,500 feet a second gave the least deflection and no blowup. Second, a bullet weight in the neighborhood of 150-grain, or heavier, is indicated. Third, all these requirements can be met with the most commonly used deer rifle calibers, either by using handloads, or factory loaded cartridges. These calibers may be any one of the following: .30/06, .280 Remington, .270 Winchester, the .30/30 Winchester, .35 Remington, .348 Winchester, .358 Winchester, 6.5X 55mm.

The velocity levels, previously indicated, should be given plenty of study in order to type in the caliber with the widest range of conditions. For example, a 150-grain bullet driven at 2,500 feet a second is excellent for heavy cover, as indicated by the tests. More to the point, this velocity would be best for the occasionally encountered longer range shot across open logging slashes, and such places, where the yardage may well open to around 250 yards or so. There would be less bullet drop over the longer distance, even with the rifle sighted in to hit point-of-aim at 100 yards, as it should be for heavy cover.

All the various actions previously discussed have complementing calibers and bullet weights at this 2,500 feet a second muzzle velocity. The essential ballistic factor a deer hunter must keep constantly in mind is that ultra-high velocity cannot be used effectively. Bullet velocity for average short-range heavy-cover shooting is very limited by the type of shots afforded. You have, on many occasions, to buck brush for a killing shot.

The shape of the bullet from round nose to spitzer point proved of less importance than I supposed at the beginning of the tests. Both the spitzer point and the round nose turned in good performances when they were of proper weight, driven at the best velocity level. That's all.

Chapter 3

Long-Range

Deer

Rifles

I AM not a one-gun man. I doubt if any deer hunter can be, if his hunting is divided between extremely long-range and short-range brush shooting. I realize, of course, that a rifleman can easily reach a compromise with some calibers, being fairly well armed for short heavy-cover shooting and for shooting at the longer ranges. But compromise it is, all along the line, from bullet weight and velocity to caliber, to sighting equipment, to rifle weight. The .30/06 comes readily to mind, with a 150 grain bullet driven at 3,000 feet a second for the long-range open shooting. In this same caliber a 180-grain bullet at 2,400 feet a second is a good brush load. In the main, however, full coverage from short to long range requires two distinct rifles, varying in weight by at least a pound.

Old woodsmen who do their deer hunting with just one rifle, usually equipped with very primitive sights, claiming full and efficient coverage on game from 50 to 350 yards are amiable old frauds. They use one rifle for all their deer hunting needs through force of circumstance. Al Lyman, hunting partner, trapper, and fly fisherman, is no exception. He owns and uses a 30/40 Krag carbine won in a poker game from a noble Redskin. This is his all-around deer rifle, but not exactly cherished.

In a world cluttered with material possessions, Al Lyman "goes light." He has one change of clothing, on and off. He has, usually, a broken box of 180-grain soft points for his Krag. These, with about 150 traps, a hunting knife redolent of skunk and raccoon, constitute his visible assets,—if you discount his cozy, tumbledown shack hid on a lumber company's reforesting and his coastal shack near the seaward dunes close to the clam flats and good Black Brant shooting. Waterfowling is a ritual to which he attends with a very ancient double-barrel Parker shotgun.

He has cursed his Krag up one side of the barrel and down the other. Off-season he thumbs through all the latest catalogues of the various custom and semi-custom sporter suppliers, reading the merits of modern, long-range deer rifles.

He wants, and needs, another deer rifle for the more open shooting, but not to the extent he would put out the labor required to buy one. Pin him down and he can outline the requirements to perfection, the exact ballistics required out where the game stands at those long ranges. He'll even tell you the exact location of the hunting grounds where this long-range paragon of a rifle could be used effectively,—across those wide, open West Coast logging slashes. He knows just how much velocity is required, with its consequent bullet drop out at 350 yards.

"Next year, Spud, you'll see me out on Bone Mountain with one of them Gibbs 30 Magnums," he tells me. "I know where there is some good gold pocket mining over toward Rogue River for this summer, muskrat trapping come winter—"

But alas for Al's good intention. When he gets as much as ten dollars together, above stark necessities, he loses it in a poker game. Once, when I suggested he make a down payment on this ideal long-range rifle he wanted to supplement his Krag's obvious brush virtues as a deer rifle, he explained it this way, "Got to buy some grub. Winter coming, and you know, Spud, even them mice are leaving my cupboard because there isn't enough victuals to keep them from going hungry."

So Al, like any number of woodsmen, will probably never, implement his dreams of having a second rifle for long-range deer shooting. He is a two-gun man forced by the fell clutch of circumstance to confine his deer hunting to just one rifle. He gets around this by hunting territory best suited to his rifle's ranging limitations, an expedient I have never liked.

I like an exacting matching of rifle capabilities to the type of deer hunting I am doing. This, obviously, means two deer rifles, for you cannot have a rifle which is *best* for brush shooting, and *best* for long-range coverage out to a full 350 yards.

If *my* cupboard becomes too bare for the mice, they are on their own. I'll settle for my second deer rifle, especially selected for long-range work.

I have used such a rifle for the past several years. During the process of getting exactly the type of rifle I wanted for open shooting, any number of calibers were tested at my benchrest and afield.

The problem of long-range shooting is essentially that of short-range brush requirements. The only difference is that these ballistics must be delivered to target at several times the ranges of those where most deer fall in heavy cover. This latter puts an entirely different emphasis on the requirements, to the point, quite often, where some of the experts are caught in a tangled web of ballistics loaded with contradictions.

Many recommendations for out-and-out long-range deer shooting by these self-appointed experts are based on muzzle ballistics. Out where the deer stand for those long-range shots, many of these recommended rifles deliver less punch than the old .30/30 Winchester at 50 yards woods ranges with a 170-grain bullet pushed at a muzzle velocity of 2,200 feet a second. Indeed, many of these highly touted calibers are not as efficient at these longer ranges as this ancient .30/30 is at woods ranges because the bullet jackets are thicker to stand those initial high muzzle velocities. After these bullets have cooled off out at 300 yards, they are light weight frauds, ambling along at very modest velocities. I name but one at this point, the .243 Winchester, 100-grain bullet, driven at a muzzle velocity of 3,070 feet a second, and a remaining velocity at 300 yards of 2,320 feet a second, a remaining energy of 1,190 foot pounds. A hunter, to be best equipped for 300-350 yards shooting must either up the bullet weight of this load, or up the velocity. It's flat shooting enough, so it is actually best to consider some calibers with more bullet weight.

I lingered a long time over the .280 Remington. Drive a 150-grain bullet at a muzzle velocity of 2,900 feet a second, as is done in this caliber, and it arrives at the 300-yard mark with a retained velocity of 2,210 feet a second—good old .30/30 ballistics at short woods ranges.

I am not one to believe that the venerable .30/30 wounds as many deer as is commonly supposed, or it wouldn't have survived as a medium-range deer rifle all these years. Obviously, thousands of hunters have found its ballistics sufficient for all short-range brush shooting. And, if these same ballistics can be delivered at 300 yards with another rifle, one cannot question its efficiency on deer-sized targets.

Delivering .30/30 ballistics out at 300 yards, though, is a task not too many of the much touted long-range rifles can achieve. The .280 Remington is a good selection, make no doubt of that. But is it the best possible selection for this range bracket? The 7mm Ackley Magnum, which drives a 160-grain bullet at a muzzle velocity of 3,125 feet a second, is a better choice from the standpoint of delivered ballistics.

Note, please, that this muzzle velocity of 3,000 to 3,200 is about tops for a 150-grain bullet in .280 caliber. Above this velocity you get plenty of barrel erosion, plenty of everything save a measurable increase in killing power. At the above mentioned velocity level, with 150-grain bullet, the 7mm delivers 1,400 to 1,500 pounds of energy, sufficient for your purpose, though a bit more wouldn't be amiss.

The .264 Winchester Magnum pushes a 140-grain bullet at a muzzle velocity of 3,180 feet a second. At 300 yards this bullet has a remaining velocity of 2,480 feet a second, with a remaining energy of 1,910 pounds. Sighted to hit point-of-aim at 225 yards, it shoots flat enough to always be on target out to 325 yards.

Several other manufacturers or importers have their own version of the 6.5mm Magnum. Any of these would be very good choices for long-range deer shooting. Some, with handloads can produce velocities low enough for best brush performance, and are fair compromises for all-around deer shooting.

Another very good long-range rifle selection is the .270 Winchester, using a 150-grain spitzer bullet pushed at 2,900 feet a second. Sighted to hit point-of-aim at 200 yards, you are on target to a full 300 yards, assuming a 10-inch diameter vital area which you must hit on deer for a clean kill.

Turning to the 30 calibers, a hunter has several good long-range choices in either wildcat or factory versions—probably the best, most efficient long-range deer calibers of the lot. I use a .300

Short Ackley Magnum wildcat. Shells are made by setting back the shoulder on the belted 300 H and H Magnum. They are cut to length. The final process is to size them by fire forming—firing a round which expands them to perfect rifle chamber fit.

The entire process, while requiring time, is not complicated. Few shells are lost in fire forming them for this wildcat caliber. After this routine the cartridges are good for several reloadings. I note the process here in order to demonstrate that there are reloading requirements for the several wildcats. You load *all* your ammo for a wildcat caliber, but beyond that there is no great handicap to owning and using such an individual rifle.

This .300 Short Ackley Magnum is superbly accurate. The cartridges are short enough to function in a standard-length bolt action—a decided advantage because it makes for less rifle weight, and the shorter bolt throw is fast for a second shot.

The very fact of this particular wildcat being ballistically in balance has several advantages. For the same velocity to bullet weight, it requires several grains less powder than the H and H Magnum with its longer, not too well formed case.

Winchester now has a factory version of a short .300 Magnum very similar to the Ackley Wildcat. This, to my way of thinking, is endorsement enough. By the same token, I regard the .300 Short Winchester Magnum as being one of the best factory long-range deer rifles. It drives a 150-grain bullet at a muzzle velocity of 3,400 feet a second. The 180-grain bullet is given a muzzle velocity of 2,890 feet a second.

By way of comparison, the .300 Short Ackley Magnum pushes a 150-grain bullet at 3,250 feet a second. The 180-grain bullet is given a muzzle velocity of 3,050 feet a second. So what I have to report about the field performance of the .300 Short Ackley Magnum has application when the .300 Short Winchester Magnum is considered.

With a rifle weight not to exceed 8½ pounds, slightly heavier than the ideal weight for a brush rifle, recoil is not at all unpleasant. This is true of all the long-range calibers considered.

It seems fitting to go into the factors of long-range rifle selection which conditioned my endorsement of the .300 Short Ackley Magnum. I am especially concerned because the ballistics of this rifle are so well fitted to long range, 300 to 350 yards. And if these ranges seem comparatively short when measured against some of the reported 500-yard kills, even with a .44 Magnum handgun, I can only plead a ballistic *nolo contendere.* After all, I am a rifle realist, prone to discount accuracy achievement afield which cannot be duplicated even at benchrest.

So, in examining the merits of this particular rifle, I make one qualification at this point. Some hunters who are ultra sensitive to recoil, might turn in a better performance with a rifle somewhat less powerful. But they cannot, in the very nature of long-range deer killing requirements, deviate much from these indicated bullet weights and velocities. Best solution of this particular recoil problem is to up the weight of the gun by one pound, even though it makes the rifle less portable, and more tiring to carry during a full day's hunt. Upping the weight of the rifle by a pound makes a slight contribution to accuracy for those long-range, precise bullet placements. And that is all to the good.

Any .30 caliber cartridge begins to loose ballistic efficiency very fast after a top loading of 70 grains of powder is exceeded. Sure, you can use an overbore capacity case and keep pouring in the fuel to up velocities. You can push a .30 caliber, 150-grain bullet at 3,700 feet a second. But all this is achieved by very short barrel life, and less than maximum accuracy.

My .300 Short Ackley Magnum has an exact powder capacity of 70 grains. It has a 28 degree shoulder on a belted case, with a length of 2.45 inches—ideal for a standard bolt-action rifle. These cartridge measurements for the .300 Short Magnum are about par for the course, wildcat or factory rifle.

Consider a moment some of the bullet requirements for clean killing at long range, deer being the quarry. You'll find them, as previously stated, very much the same as for short-range brush shooting. (A) Expansion without blowup at all game ranges from 100 to 350 yards. In the .300 Short Magnum this expansion will be around 70 to 80 caliber. (B) Good penetration. This requirement, as you know, indicates a fairly heavy bullet. For not all, or even most, of the deer stand in those classic poses so beloved of magazines and book illustrators. They often present quartering shots requiring as much as 25 to 30 inches of penetration *before* touching the vital chest area. You cannot have immediate blowup and clean, one-shot kills under such circumstances. (C) Good trajectory, with little bullet drop. This item should be read forward and backward. Put the slipstick on the proposi-

Long-range deer shooting has many of the elements of short-range shooting, but usually there is an opportunity to get into a steady position, such as is exemplified here.

tion, with those previously mentioned range brackets in mind, plus required penetration for a clean kill, and you come up with a rather startling ballistic conclusion. Maybe, though, it isn't so startling or unorthodox after all, depending on the school of rifle shooting to which you belong. The requirements spell out a fairly heavy bullet, with excellent sectional density and ballistic coefficient. In the .30 caliber a 180-grain spitzer point is indicated. In the smaller calibers, starting with the 6.5mm it should be at least 140—150 grain is better, especially in the .270, and the .280 Remington, regular or Magnum, the 7mm Magnums, all at a velocity of around 2,900 to 3,200 feet a second.

Note, please, that nothing has been said about nerve shock in connection with this long-range killing. Nerve shock is a beloved factor of high velocity, "blow 'em up" gunbugs. But after having killed literally hundreds of deer I cannot subscribe unreservedly to this theory. A disruption of a vital area is an important factor in a clean kill, caused by good penetration and expansion with its consequent destruction of tissue. Shock is good, but it must always be subordinate to these other primary requirements.

When some expert talks learnedly about complete bullet energy utilization, with the expanded bullet caught beneath the hide on the off side of some luckless buck, I am a sucker for such learned hair splitting. But if my own extended deer-hunting experience is of any worth, it indicates a contrary conclusion. I'll trade some of that completely utilized energy for a good wide exit wound. And this type wound channel is made with a fairly heavy bullet which expands to a maximum diameter, then plows on through, regardless of how the deer is positioned for the shot.

Here are some range figures for the 300 Short Ackley Magnum, a caliber which is very typical of several wildcats and factory rifles of this bore size.

TRAJECTORY*

100 yards	200 yards	300 yards	350 yards
1½″+	0	6″—	12″—

Muzzle	100 yards	200 yards	300 yards
V.3025	2800	2580	2400
E.3600	3130	2621	2300

V. = Velocity in foot second.   E. = Energy in foot pounds.

* 180-grain bullet.

35—Long-Range Deer Rifles

When the ballistics of this 180-grain .30-caliber bullet are disregarded, the question arises about the use of a 150-grain bullet driven at even a higher velocity and perhaps flatter trajectory over the course. And a very good ballistic argument could be put up for this lighter bullet. But bullet weight, to the limits of required trajectory and drop over extended ranges stem from the same considerations as those required to a great extent for short-range brush shooting, where bullet deflection is always a prime consideration. One must measure the ballistics out where the game stands in long-range shooting.

Quite often I have taken shots at mule deer which stood partly screened by juniper, sagebrush or bitterbrush. A shot may be at 125 yards; it may be at a full 350, but in any event the bullet must be angled in through a brush screening, just as it is in short-range heavy-cover shooting at 50 yards or so. And here, as in the short-range brush shooting, the heavier bullet, after velocity has been reduced by distance, has less deflection.

I recall the first deer I downed with a .300 Short Magnum. I hunted a large western logging slash coming lush to a new reforesting. Al Lyman, carrying his Krag Carbine, paced me on these comparatively open ridges. Hearing my shot he came across the draw to critically examine my deer. The range, actually was a modest 125 yards, very short for a specialized deer rifle of this nature. But the late evening didn't make it any setup. My three-point buck was completely obscured by a large fir stump, save for a bit of neck and head. In the fast fading evening light I managed to clip him behind the ear from an off-hand position.

That 180-grain, .30 caliber bullet, moving along faster than its ideal performance bracket of 2,500 to 2,200 feet a second at the target, reacted violently. The velocity at this point would be in the 2,750 feet-a-second bracket, a bit higher than required for a clean kill with a body hit; and it might be added, a bit high for the best in penetration. But tack on another 100 to 200 yards of range and it would be sufficiently cooled down to turn in a top-hole performance.

Al Lyman turned over the three pointer and looked at it. "Not bad," he said. "But iffen I was buying one of them long-range deer rifles it wouldn't be no .300 Short Ackley Magnum, no sir. Give me a .30 Gibbs."

I wanted to tell Al how my old math professor claimed there were always two right answers to any problem, but I kept my counsel. Our hunting rucksacks were cached behind a windfall a good quarter mile away across the logging slash, and they contained our trail lights. With night fast approaching, those lights were an immediate concern to find our way back to camp.

Besides, when you have the heft of a good buck on your back, the rifle in hand with which you killed it, you are apt to be charitable about other deer rifle calibers and other hunters' opinions. My mellowness might have been ascribed to the October full moon touching the rim of the western sky on this occasion. But I felt it came from having a rifle matched to my long-range deer hunting requirements, a small but important segment of the sport.

Even at the expense of repeating myself, those long-range requirements need to be restated. They are: a bullet drop of not more than 10 to 12 inches at 350 yards, with the rifle sighted to hit point-of-aim at 200 to 225 yards, a bullet weight of not less than 140 grains with a remaining energy of 1,550 foot pounds at 300 yards, 1,800 foot pounds being even better. It should have a remaining velocity of not less than 2,200 feet a second at this distance.

Matching these requirements to the available calibers is comparatively simple. Sometimes, with certain modern calibers, it is a matter of a special handload for a rifle normally used with other ammunition for brush shooting. In the main, however, I think that this matching is most closely approached for long-range shooting with a .264 Winchester Magnum, a .270 Winchester, a .280 Remington in the standard or Magnum version, the several 7mm wildcat calibers, all using a 150-grain bullet. The .300 Short Winchester Magnum, the .300 Short Ackley Magnum, and several versions of this particular gun, are better served with a 180-grain bullet. All these are splendid long-range deer rifles.

Chapter 4

Iron Sights
for Brush-Shooting
Deer Rifles

SNAPSHOOTING. Heavy cover. Short ranges. Limited time for a shot. These place plenty of emphasis on deer rifle sights. They especially underscore the need for proper iron sights in the touch and go of average woods shooting. There are many more right answers to the problem of proper deer calibers for short-range brush shooting than there are to the problem of proper iron sights. The element of time, making basic demands on a brush rifle, places even more emphasis on proper sights. There is a woodman's saying to the effect that all deer hunters must lose a chance at a trophy buck at least once before becoming fully conscious of this sight problem.

Here we are concerned with iron sights alone. But by the same token, we must be concerned with the ranges at which they deliver their best performance. Let's place the range limitations at not more than 150 yards. Beyond this distance, obviously, a basic element of precision enters the picture to the point where a scope sight is to be preferred. Beyond a distance of around 200 yards the problem of the best rifle for the long-range bracket enters the picture. Out to around 200 yards, however, those rifles previously considered for brush shooting, using bullets at a muzzle velocity of 2,500 feet a second, all turn in acceptable performances to this yardage. But here the problem is actually one of sights in combination—iron and scope sights.

Iron sight alone, however, have a very well defined place in short-range, woods shooting. Indeed, with a properly stocked rifle, designed for the exacting task of accurate offhand shooting, no sights at all, or just a front sight can prove startlingly efficient. For one always has an element of rifle pointing as well as aiming in this fast, slight-of-hand shooting, much the same as an upland shotgun is handled.

Few iron sights, as they come from the manufacturer, have any merit to recommend them to the serious deer hunter. They must be modified in many instances before they can be considered field efficient. Take front sights as an example. You can have a round gold bead, an ivory bead, and there are a few made of red or white plastic. You have a choice of a round face, a flat faced bead or one set at an angle to catch the skylight. Formerly there was a front sight with a small mirror to reflect the strong skylight and angle it onto the bead, but of recent years I haven't seen one of these advertised.

Bead size may run from an average of 1/16 to ⅛ inch in diameter. It is seldom, however, that any bead size is considered in reference to barrel length. They are placed on all lengths of barrels from a short 18 inches to a long 26 inches, willy-nilly. They are seldom considered in reference to proper receiver sight aperture when such a rear sight is used.

But all these factors of proper sight fitting are important, much beyond the casual attention usually given them. For each segment of deer shooting accuracy at short range must have its inception in these sight considerations. Attended to, they contribute directly to a confident shot when you have a chance at a trophy buck.

The basic problem of front bead size to barrel length is easily stated, and it has application for all iron sights. *The center of interest and the intended center of bullet impact must coincide.* Spelled out this means that anything in the way of sighting equipment which, even momentarily, detracts from target attention is wrong as rain at a picnic.

This deer target is your primary interest, first, last, and all the time. It is usually not waiting around, and places a premium on all the fast, off-hand accuracy you can muster. A large, conspicuous front sight so often recommended—one with a ⅛-inch white bead, on a short 20-inch barrel, will subtend enough to make the vital area of a deer appear small, hard to hit. Quite often it will completely cover the essential target. Even with a deer rifle having a 24- to 26-inch barrel, this bead is entirely too large for fast, accurate shooting at short range.

Brilliance in a sight cannot be ignored, of course. For the requirement of having a bead which is instantly caught in aiming, without distracting from the center of interest which is always the target, is a must. This brilliance, however, should be compounded of proper bead shape and proper bead color. A small bead can meet all these conditions much better than a large bead which is dependent on size for its eye-catching appeal.

Specifically, if you are using a deer rifle with not more than a 20-inch barrel, regardless of the type of action, I doubt if any bead larger than 1/16 inch makes any contribution to either speed or accuracy. If you have a deer rifle with a 24-inch barrel, you may increase this size slightly. Beads much larger than 1/16 inch in diameter can very easily break up the required close rifle-hunter relationship on a fast brush shot, and there is a falling away of expected accuracy.

This brush accuracy, incidentally, is measured not only by the size of the group produced, but by the speed with which just *one* shot can be delivered to a moving target. Here, as in the selection of a rifle for brush shooting, you must consider the limited time allowed for the shot. For when a deer is not moving, there is always the threat of movement, so target range deliberation is out, just as target range sights are out.

In selecting a bead for a 20- to 22-inch barreled rifle, 1/16 inch is an excellent size. Gold color is probably your best bet, too. Under the very different light conditions of bare ground, the forest splashed with the crimsons of autumn, to snow laden trees, a gold colored bead always stands out. The ivory or white bead, while acceptable for bare-ground hunting, does have a tendency to blend in with the snow.

When a gold bead is selected, and I believe it is your best choice, there are several things which you may do to improve its basic good qualities. First, the rounded top of a bead can make its contribution to high and low shooting under adverse light conditions of a forest under storm. Second, even the gold color of this bead can be canceled out in late evening because it doesn't catch all the available light. These objections, however, are easily overcome.

Take a small file and flatten the top of the bead. This will correct the tendency of the sight to vary elevation under different light conditions. The face of the bead can be sloped back at an angle to catch the skylight by careful filing. When you have made these two simple alterations, your rifle takes on something of a fast handling upland shotgun. Snap it to your shoulder now and that altered bead stands out in vision under all light conditions. It is small enough to be subordinate to the target, yet conspicuous enough to be easily picked up for a fast shot.

You should test your sights under the poorest light condition you are apt to find while hunting. See how it looks in late evening, a time when you may be watching some favorite feeding area. You may wish to use a slightly different bead size, due to the peculiarity of your eyesight. Don't hesitate to change.

Start with the next size larger bead, a 3/32-inch diameter. Work it down in the manner just mentioned. Test. Try. It's possible you may want a greater angle to the bead to catch more skylight. It's possible you'll want to make both sides of the bead square to complement the square top line. Do any of these things suggested to you by your actual testing on your rifle. For no two individuals see in quite the same manner, and this idiosyncrasy must be taken into consideration if the full potential of your rifle sights are to be realized.

Some riflemen, using a 24-inch barrel gun for their brush shooting, use a bead as large as 3/16 *after* it is properly shaped. For these gunners I recommend the Redfield Sourdough, square gold bead sight, set at 45 degree angle to catch the skylight. I have always felt, however, that this particular sight has too large a bead for any rifle with a barrel shorter than 24 inches. If it could be had with a square 1/16-inch gold bead for the shorter, 20- to 22-inch barreled deer rifles, it would cover just about all woods shooting requirements.

After selecting a proper bead, there is yet a rear sight to be considered. I am going to list just one aperture sight which can be had for any type rifle along with a side glance at another sight not available, save for the splendid line of bolt action Husqvarna rifles.

It would seem that with the large army of deer hunters using iron sights, and with the aperture receiver sight getting the nod from most of these hunters, more effort would be made to give then a good receiver sight. But this hasn't been done. The larger share of aperture receiver sights offered are those which had their inspiration in target shooting. They are cluttered with knobs beyond the telling. They all need streamlining. And, while they are excellent sights for target shooting, they are something less than best for short-range deer shooting.

The one exception to this is the William's Foolproof receiver sight. Here is the one receive sight with an uncluttered deck. The only thing above the cross-bar is the aperture, itself, I recommend this sight if you plan on using a receiver sight. It has good adjustments for both windage and elevation, and once your deer rifle is sighted in, those adjustments are not easily turned by some curious hunter. They are not easily knocked out afield either.

The other receiver sight mentioned before is the *Cascade Snap-shooter* which I had a modest part in designing and testing afield. This sight sets directly on the bridge of the Husqvarna Mauser rifle, imported by Tradewinds, Inc. It utilizes the two holes drilled for a top mounted scope. Small, with nothing above the bridge of the sight save the aperture stem, it carries both windage and elevation adjustments. This is a very efficient sight for a snapshooting deer rifle.

In using a receiver sight, you must always keep in mind proper aperture size. It is always better to err on the side of a too large aperture, if this is possible, than to try and use one with a very small hole. For average short-range deer shooting you should have an aperture of .095 to .125 inches. The woodsman's rule for iron sight is: *keep the front bead small, the rear aperture large.* And that has much to recommend it.

The rim of the aperture disk shouldn't carry too much metal. If you have an aperture of .125 inches, with an over-all diameter of the disk of 3/8 inches you are well served. Some experienced deer hunters do not care for even this much rim about their aperture sight disk. Many of them often throw away the disk entirely, and use the basic aperture on the sight.

This procedure, under certain light conditions, can slow the shot for some individuals. For the rim of the aperture simply disappears. Yet, if you do not need the reassurance a heavy dark ring about your aperture, such as a disk gives, you are not hampered with this seeming disappearance.

Using a well fitted rifle, and being able to disregard the rear aperture rim, you will find that the bead is invariably centered, regardless. Here, as in testing for bead size, you should experiment to see how *your* eyes respond to such a sight.

Open sights for short-range deer shooting? Why not? After all, open sights got the nod from an older generation of woodsmen who had much more experience deer shooting than any modern hunter can hope to have. Many so-called experts downgrade open sights on deer rifles. They point out that these sights have few, if any, adjustments for windage and elevation; that they are very inaccurate, and the hunter is much better served with an aperture receiver sight. More, they are quick to say that you must achieve the impossible of trying to focus your eyes on three objectives at three different distances at the same time—rear sight, front sight, target.

None of these contentions is true. First, open sights are not inaccurate to the extent that you might lose a deer by wounding or missing, where a scope sight or a receiver sight would enable you to make the kill. As for the adjustments, these are sufficient on open sight to allow you to sight your rifle in. Beyond this, adjustments on a hunter rifle have little merit.

More, open sights are perhaps the fastest to align of any. Proof of this is the very fact that most exhibition shooters use open sights for their aerial targets and the English prefer open sights for close-range shooting of dangerous African game—all of which seems recommendation enough.

Using open sights, you look *over* the rear sight, *past* the front sight, with your vision focused on the target. No optical impossibility is required, as some of the previously mentioned experts contend. You do *not* try to focus your eyes on both sights and the target at one and the same time. For good open sights are used in the *same* manner as you would use an aperture sight, save that you look *through* the aperture and *past* the front sight to the center of interest, your target.

This is the manner in which woodsmen have always used open sights. Those whom I have known intimately were deadly deer shots in the woods. One, I recall, took seventeen deer with 20 cartridges. No setup shots, nothing save the ability to use the open sights on his old, beat out Model 94 Winchester Carbine lever-action. This hunter ran a pack of "cat" hounds, devoting full time to hunting Mountain Lion and Bobcat which preyed on the deer herds. He had a state permit to kill the required number of deer to feed his hounds and himself while afield. He did this with a minimum of effort.

Best of the available open sights, it seems to me, are those made by Marbles Arms Company. You have a choice of a flat top sight, semi-buckhorn, and full buckhorn. My recommendation is the flat top, with its white diamond.

All in all, the outlined requirements for fitting your deer rifle with iron sights give you plenty of leeway in your selection. But select you must, with meticulous attention to your individual eye requirements. If you find open sights more natural for your style of shooting, then by all means select them. It's the same way with bead size. After all it is you who will be behind that rifle when your trophy buck goes out, and you want every detail right for the occasion—from your individual viewpoint.

I have simply outlined some of the considerations about which you must be acutely conscious when you are shaping up your rifle for deer hunting.

There is yet another consideration to all this sight selection, iron and scope sights in combination. But this, along with a consideration of scope sight selection, is the subject of the next chapter.

Chapter 5

Scope Sights

for

Deer Rifles

FOR woods hunting, long-range open-country shooting, you can well ponder the desirability of scope sights for your deer rifle. This scope may be used as a supplement to your iron sights in the brush. It may also be used alone. In either event there must be a careful matching of scope to the type shooting, along with proper scope mounts. Not just any power scope is best for deer shooting any more than all-type iron sights deliver top shooting performance. Here, as with *all* shooting, there is a segment of specialization underscoring the very critical selection.

When you are using a scope sight for brush shooting, you have probably, if you are an average hunter, considered the field of view in reference to 100 yards. This is not realistic. A 4X glass usually has a 30-foot field of view at this distance. A few 4X's have as much as 34 feet. In this relatively large field at 100 yards a running deer is easily picked up and contained for the shot. But, suppose you are hunting heavy cover and jump your deer at 25 yards. He has another 25 yards to go before vanishing in a heavy screening of snow laden huckleberry brush. What happens to that 100-yard, 30-foot field of your 4X scope?

The Indian carry, a fine way to be handling a rifle when one must get into action immediately.

FIELD OF VIEW IN FEET

Power	25 yards	50 yards	100 yards
6X	5.2	10.5	21.0
4X	7.5	15.0	30.0
3X	10.0	20.0	40.0
2½X	11.5	23.0	46.0
1½X	15.2	31.0	62.0

That deer, smoking out of its bead at 25 yards, with only another 25 yards to go before canceling out an opportunity for a shot, how does it stack up against the fields of view in the 25-yard column of the above chart? With a scope having a 6X magnification you would have a plenty hard time getting him in your field of view— and a much greater job keeping him there for the shot. The 6X would give you slightly more than a 5-foot field of view, almost an impossible setup with this power. Yet, I have met deer hunters in heavy cover with rifles scoped with 6X glass sights.

Suppose, though, you drop down to a 4X scope, same deer, same 25-yard range. You would have a few more feet of field, but not much. With a deer moving slowly or standing, a 4X scope would give you a shot under all light conditions, provided the objective lens of this 4X are 20mm or larger in diameter. A fast deer, however, would prove a very difficult problem.

Take the time I hunkered down in the salal brush while Elzie Randolph and Bucky McKay did a still hunting drive toward me. There were plenty of deer in that over-grown reforesting. Bucks had hooked the small trees and huckleberry brush. They had left their great splay-footed tracks in the wet clay of the deer trails crisscrossing the reforesting.

I sat, back to a small sheltering fir, watching a point where three deer trails converged from the section where Bucky and Elzie still hunted. This morning I carried a rifle equipped with a 4X scope having a generous 34-foot field at 100 yards, a boss instrument for the more open ridges which we had hunted just after good shooting light this morning. But now, with ranges closed to 25 to 35 yards in the heavy reforesting, it was no premium. Actually, I should have removed it and depended on my iron sights.

Instead, I sat there, my attention undividedly on that intersection of deer trails. A maple leaf ticked down through the silent cover as the scarlet autumn trees stirred to a beginning of the morning thermal wind change. Far away across the ridges I could hear the lonesome hammering of a woodpecker. Then this deer, a big three pointer, was on the trail moving fast, his ivory tipped antlers agleam in the weak wash of morning sun.

I snapped my rifle up, saw what I took to be a shoulder, and touched off the shot. Range? Twenty-five yards! I worked the bolt, tried for a second shot, but my deer had vanished in the vine maple, I listened to his running, totally disappointed. I thought I heard an alien note in his rhythmic running, even thought I heard a low crash. Then there was silence.

I looked at my nicely scoped rifle. I thought of its splendid potential for making those comparatively long shots across logging slashes, area watching shots when I had an old orchard under observation during a long evening. What I needed here in this heavy cover was a scope of not more than $2\frac{1}{2}$X with a wide field of view. A power around $1\frac{1}{2}$X would be even better. Resolution and definition were no problem. Here, as in most short-range shooting the problem was field of view.

After Elzie and Bucky converged on my stand, I took up the trail of the big three pointer, then came upon him about 50 yards from the point where I made the shot. The bullet had caught him a bit too far back for an immediate kill. I wasn't proud of this shot by any means. With a little less luck it could have been a superficial wounding hit. At this short range, with a proper scope sight, I could see no good reason why I couldn't have broken his neck. I have brought off such shots many times before, and have done it since this occurrence, both with iron sights and with scoped deer rifles.

A tendency of many hunters to equip their brush rifles with 4X scopes suggests a basic rule for your consideration: use no more power than you must for a field of view around 46 feet at 100 yards. This would indicate a scope power of not more than $2\frac{1}{2}$X— a $1\frac{1}{2}$X would be even better.

To get this in perspective, it is well to consider some of the requirements in detail, along with the peculiarities of eyesight which must always be taken to consideration in making an intelligent selection of deer rifle hunting scopes.

The exit pupil of a scope governs the amount of light reaching the eye of the viewer. This light, actually, is a factor of objective lens diameter in connection with exit pupil size. The human eye, under adverse light conditions, can adjust to about 5 millimeters, accommodating this amount of light from a scope during late evening or early morning, to say nothing of dark overcast days in heavy cover. During the strong light of midday, the human eye adjusts to around 2.5 millimeters.

All this adds up to the very pertinent fact that a scope exit pupil much larger than 5 millimeters transmits more light than can be used by the viewer. But, by the same token, a requirement of at least 5 millimeters *is* indicated for all hunting scopes for complete coverage.

Next, consider relative brightness, the least understood of the several factors making a direct contribution to scope sight efficiency. Relative brightness must not be confused with magnification or image quality. It refers directly to exit pupil area, and is the square of the exit pupil.

A scope with an objective lens of 20 millimeters, rated as a 4X, has an exit pupil of 5 millimeters. This squared $5 \times 5 = 25$, the relative brightness. Up the power of this scope to 6X, with no corresponding change in the 20 millimeter objective lens and the relative brightness is decreased to about 11.08, and the exit pupil is 3.33 millimeters—unacceptable for poor light conditions.

To recapitulate at this point, the qualities you must look for in a proper hunting scope are: *flat field, good definition or resolution, an exit pupil of at least 5 millimeters, and its entailed relative brightness of 25. The scope must have positive, minute of angle adjustments for both elevation and windage.* It must be weather proof and the lens should be coated.

Weather proofing and coated optics may be taken for granted in any of the better quality scopes. There are other scope requirements you should be familiar with in making an intelligent selection of a hunting scope for your deer shooting, but the above requirements go together to the extent that you should fix them in your mind before proceeding with the other requirements.

If you have your scope reticule centered on that trophy buck, and a slight movement of your head in reference to the exit pupil makes the target appear to shift position, you have parallax in your scope. This phenomenon is more pronounced in the higher-powered scopes. It is also more pronounced at closer ranges. But in the medium powered scopes normally used for deer shooting parallax is no great problem. I remark here, *all* scopes have some parallax. But the error of aim introduced by it at most ranges is unimportant.

You should know what parallax is, however, and any scope of questionable quality should be tested for it. This testing for excessive parallax is a simple undertaking. You align the scope on some object about 50 yards away. Hold it steady. Now move your head from side to side. If there is any great amount of apparent displacement of the target in reference to the reticule, the scope has too much parallax and shouldn't be considered for your deer rifle.

Proper selection of scope reticules is very important. Here, with the several available types on the market, you have a wide selection in buying your scope. In extensive tests here, however, I narrowed the list considerably. In reality, I found two types which gave the best definition on neutral-colored targets during late evening. One of these was a flat topped post, with crosshair. The other was a "diamond dot" and crosshair. Either of these would prove a good selection for short-range, heavy-cover, late-evening shooting.

For the longer ranges a medium fine crosshair cannot be beat. The conflicting requirements of short-range snapshooting, late-evening shooting, and the requirements of precision long-range shooting, indicate, for the most part, two scopes with some qualifications.

One of the best all-round reticule combinations for both short- and long-range shooting is to be found on the Bushnell with the *command post* reticule. This, as you probably know, is a two-way combination: post and crosshair, or crosshair alone.

The post crosshair of the Bushnell can be erected for late evening or early morning shooting or for cloudy days in heavy cover by a simple adjustment on the side of the scope tube. For longer range, more precise shooting, it can be folded down and the crosshairs used alone. This is an almost perfect solution for a deer hunter using one rifle for both his woods shooting and long-range rifle work.

The "Diamond Dot" reticule is an exclusive of the Tradewinds Scopes. This dot, instead of being a conventional round shape, has a very distinct, clear-cut diamond outline at the junction of the crosshairs. In tests on actual deer targets I found this superior to the conventional round dot for late evening shooting.

There is no need to tell you to select a scope with proper eye relief. Anyone of the several quality makes available has correct eye relief, running from 3 to 4 inches, which is ample for all your requirements. Eye relief, as you know, is the distance the eye is placed from the exit lens for a full field of view.

Variable power scopes are manufactured or imported by several firms. Bausch and Lomb, Bushnell, Tradewinds, Leupold, Redfield, all come to mind. There are others. These firms all have a very typical approach to the problem, with most of their scopes having power options from 2½ to 9X, with one exception. Field of view are from around 42 feet, with the lower power option, to around 18 feet at the highest setting—100 yards. Scope weights of these variable powers are around 13.5 ounces.

The one exception noted above is the Tradewinds TW-Zoom 1½ to 4X variable power. This is an exciting new concept in deer hunting scopes which I believe is more versatile than the average. With the 1½X setting you have a relative brightness of 144, *and* a field of view at 100 yards of 64 feet. This can be translated into shooting in heavy cover where you often take a shot at a fast-moving target not more than half this distance: the field of view at 50 yards is a full 32 feet and 16 feet at 25 yards.

This Tradewinds TW-Zoom 1½ to 4X variable power is a very neat scope, with an eye adjustment that is especially good. With the 4X power option it is an excellent instrument for the longer range shooting. In tests here I found it exceptionally good for late evening shooting with the setting at 1½X, giving about fifteen minutes more shooting light than other scopes with higher power.

After selecting a scope for your deer rifle (I think it might well be a variable power, especially this Tradewinds TW-Zoom 1½ to 4X), you have the problem of a proper mount. Quite frequently, if you hunt the full deer season, there will be times when the weather indicates the use of iron sights for your short-range shooting—any shooting as a matter of fact. For example, when there is a real old stinker of a storm growling across your happy hunting grounds, it is iron sights or nothing.

Under the circumstances you have the choice of removing your scope completely, or of using swing mounts to get it out of the way of iron sights. My thought is that when storm does cancel out a scope sight, it is best removed entirely and placed either in the protection of your hunting rucksack or shooting jacket. Removed, it leaves the rifle uncluttered for your shooting. With the swing mounts and the scope held to one side for iron sight use, the rifle is out of balance. And quite often the unemployed scope obscures your field of view.

Quick detachable mounts for your scope solve this problem neatly. When they are employed the scope can be removed within a minute. When it is replaced it always goes back to the previously sighted-in zero. Among the several very good mounts presently available, I can recommend Herkner's Echo Side Mount. When the scope is removed, using this mount, there is only a very small segment of mount left on the rifle. Another very good solution to this problem is the Williams Quick Detachable Mount.

I use the Echo side mount on one of my rifles with the scope mounted to just clear a Tradewinds Snapshooter aperture sight. The scope must be removed to use this sight. But once removed the iron sights need no adjustment before use. This arrangement has worked out wonderfully well, making for a very versatile rifle, often used for woods hunting with iron sights, and with scope sights when I am prowling the large logging slashes of my Happy Hunting Grounds. The rifle is often used, too, for late evening area watching, the scope in place.

With the Williams Quick Detachable Mount, used on another of my deer rifles, the scope base remains directly on the receiver when the glass is removed. This base serves as the foundation for a Williams Ace-in-the-Hole peep sight when the scope is removed, an operation which takes only a minute. The peep sight disk is sighted in separately and may, like the Tradewinds Snapshooter, be sighted for a range entirely different than that for which the scope is sighted. And it, like the scope, returns to its particular zero setting when it is replaced after the scope is removed.

Some deer hunters, of course, will want to use open sights to supplement their scope sights. Open sights pose no problem as the scope sight can be mounted behind them. Then, when it is removed, you have your open sights ready and waiting. Any of the quick detachable scope mounts work well with these open sights.

Whatever the type and combination of iron and scope sights you use, you still have the problem of sighting in the scope for best coverage. With iron sights the usual distance at which you sight-in is to point-of-aim at 100 yards. This, ordinarily, places your bullet only about 1.5 inches high at 50 yards with most of the calibers previously discussed. But with scope sights, to get the widest possible range coverage, the best distances vary with the caliber, especially for the longer range shooting.

All maximum ranges should be touched upon in sighting in your deer rifle with a scope, without canceling out the shorter yardages at which it may be used. In this respect it is somewhat a different problem than when you are sighting in with iron sights. For an iron sighted deer rifle is ordinarily used at the shorter ranges, and a zero of 100 yards covers all distances at which it will be normally used, from a short 25 yards out to 200 yards, with most of the shots taken at *less* than the zero setting.

With scope sights, however, you are very apt to cover *all* the ranges normally associated with iron sights in woods hunting, and also those longer ranges found in the more open shooting. More to the point, you may also be using a specially selected rifle for the more open shooting, something which has plenty of merit. And where you are readying a deer rifle for out-and-out long ranges and selecting any of the many flat shooting, modern calibers such as the 7mm Weatherby, the .280 Winchester Magnum, the splendid 7mm Remington, or other rifles having ballistics similar to the .300 Short Ackley Magnum mentioned before, your rifle should be zeroed at not less than 200 to 250 yards.

Using the very popular .30/06, 150-grain bullet at factory velocities, you can zero in at 250 yards and the bullet will take the following course: maximum trajectory height 3.6 inches. Distance to the highest trajectory point 150 yards. Distance to the point where the bullet is 4.5 inches below line of sight 300 yards. Distance to the point where the bullet is 8 inches below line of sight 325 yards. *Height above line of sight at 50 yards 1.2 inches.* Examine these figures carefully and you'll see that this sighting puts you on at *all ranges* out to 325 yards.

Something more is also indicated. That trajectory height of 1.2 above point-of-aim at 50 yards is an excellent reference point in bringing your rifle in for the longer distances. For, if you sight in at 50 yards with your bullets grouping slightly more than one inch *above* point-of-aim, you'll find it much easier to bring your rifle to taw than if this is attempted at the longer yardages.

After bringing your rifle in at 50 yards, with the bullets printing 1.2 inches or so above point-of-aim, then it is time enough to test it for the longer distances. All this, of course, with an out-and-out long-range rifle. Where you are using a rifle basically selected for the touch-and-go of woods hunting, the *maximum ranges* are slightly shorter than those of out-and-out long-range deer rifles. Under the circumstances, it is best to zero in with your scope at the shorter recommended distance of 200 yards.

Appended here is a ballistic table, courtesy *Bausch & Lomb,* with a recommended zero distance for various deer rifle calibers. This is on the basis of the bullet being within three inches *above* or *below* line of sight out to the maximum distances specified.

ZERO DISTANCES FOR CALIBERS

Cartridge	Bullet Weight in Grains	Zero in Yards	Maximum Range	Height above point-of-aim at 50 Yards in Inches
6mm Remington	100	262	306	0.9
.243 Winchester	75	269	311	0.9
.243 Winchester	80	272	316	0.8
.243 Winchester	90	254	296	0.9
.243 Winchester	100	252	294	1.0
.244 Remington	75	270	313	0.8
.244 Remington	90	254	296	0.9
.25/35 Winchester	117	181	211	1.7
.250 Savage	87	184	215	1.7
.250 Savage	100	220	257	1.3
.256 Winchester Mag.	60	198	228	1.4
6.5 Arisaka	139	214	250	1.5
6.5 Arisaka	156	179	209	1.9
6.5 Mann. Sch.	77	244	283	1.0
6.5 Mann. Sch.	156	206	242	1.4
6.5 X 55	77	244	283	1.0
6.5 X 55	93	241	279	1.0
6.5 X 55	139	245	286	1.2
6.5 X 55	156	209	245	1.4
257 Roberts	87	253	294	0.9
.257 Roberts	100	230	267	1.1
.257 Roberts	117	209	244	1.3
.257 Weatherby Mag.	87	286	330	0.7
.257 Weatherly Mag.	100	278	324	0.7
.257 Weatherby Mag.	117	258	300	0.9
.264 Winchester Mag.	100	287	334	0.7
.264 Winchester Mag.	140	273	316	1.0
.270 Weatherby Mag.	100	283	328	0.7
.270 Weatherby Mag.	130	271	316	0.8
.270 Weatherby Mag.	150	264	308	0.9

Cartridge	Bullet Weight in Grains	Zero in Yards	Maximum Range	Height above point-of-aim at 50 Yards in Inches
.270 Winchester	100	270	314	0.8
.270 Winchester	130	259	303	0.9
.270 Winchester	150	238	279	1.1
7mm Remington Mag.	150	283	330	0.9
7mm Remington Mag.	175	238	277	1.1
7mm Weatherby Mag.	139	267	312	0.9
7mm Weatherby Mag.	154	259	304	0.9
7mm Weatherby Mag.	175	250	292	1.0
7 X 57 Mauser	110	251	293	1.0
7 X 57 Mauser	150	238	276	1.3
7 X 57 Mauser	175	201	235	1.5
7 X 61 H & H	160	271	316	1.0
.280 Remington	100	277	322	0.8
.280 Remington	125	258	301	0.9
.280 Remington	150	241	282	1.1
.280 Remington	165	228	266	1.2
.284 Winchester	125	257	300	0.9
.284 Winchester	150	238	279	1.1
.30 Carbine	110	153	179	2.1
.30 Remington	170	172	201	1.8
.30/06 Springfield	110	250	289	0.9
.30/06 Springfield	125	252	293	0.9
.30/06 Springfield	130	262	305	0.9
.30/06 Springfield	150	236	275	1.1
.30/06 Springfield	180	214	249	1.3
.30/06 Springfield	220	197	230	1.5
.30/30 Winchester	150	186	216	1.6
.30/30 Winchester	160	178	207	1.7
.30/30 Winchester	170	179	209	1.7
.30/40 Krag	180	197	230	1.5
.30/40 Krag	220	185	217	1.7
.300 H. & H. Magnum	150	257	299	0.9
.300 H. & H. Magnum	180	252	293	1.1
.300 H. & H. Magnum	220	217	254	1.3
.300 Savage	150	215	251	1.3
.300 Savage	180	190	222	1.6
.300 Weatherby Mag.	110	312	361	0.5
.300 Weatherby Mag.	150	283	330	0.7
.300 Weatherby Mag.	180	265	310	0.9
7.65 Argentine	150	237	277	1.1
7.7 Arisaka	130	237	277	1.1
7.7 Arisaka	180	216	251	1.5
7.7 Arisaka	215	188	220	1.6
.303 British	130	225	263	1.2

55—Scope Sights for Deer Rifles

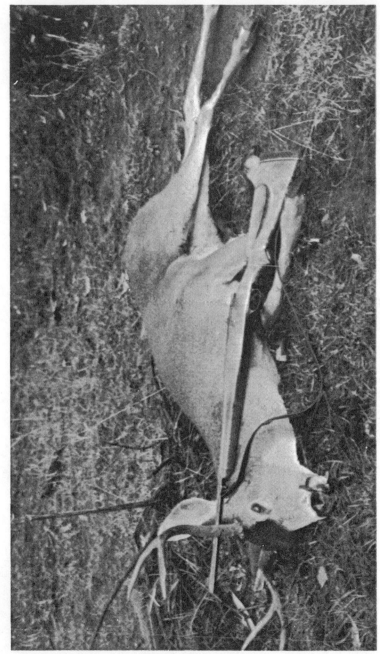

A beautiful buck taken by the author while still hunting in heavy cover.

Cartridge	Bullet Weight in Grains	Zero in Yards	Maximum Range	Height above Point-of-aim at 50 Yards in Inches
.303 British	150	221	258	1.3
.303 British	180	212	248	1.4
.303 British	215	182	213	1.7
.303 Savage	180	172	201	1.8
.303 Savage	190	161	189	2.0
.308 Norma Mag.	180	257	310	1.0
.308 Winchester	110	248	286	0.9
.308 Winchester	125	247	287	1.0
.308 Winchester	150	228	266	1.2
.308 Winchester	180	207	242	1.4
.308 Winchester	200	203	238	1.5
8 X 56 Mann. Sch.	200	178	208	1.7
8mm Lebel	170	209	243	1.4
8 X 57 Mauser	170	204	239	1.4
.32 Remington	170	168	196	1.9
.32 Winchester Special	170	179	208	1.7
.338 Winchester Mag.	200	243	285	1.1
.338 Winchester Mag.	250	221	259	1.3
.338 Winchester Mag.	300	200	234	1.5
.348 Winchester	150	214	246	1.3
.348 Winchester	200	199	232	1.5
.348 Winchester	250	186	216	1.6
.35 Remington	150	185	214	1.6
.35 Remington	200	175	204	1.8
.351 Winchester	180	151	176	2.1
.358 Norma Mag.	250	227	265	1.2
.358 Winchester	200	203	237	1.4
.358 Winchester	250	187	219	1.9
9.3 X 57	232	189	219	1.6
9.3 X 57	286	171	201	1.8
.375 H. & H. Mag.	270	236	276	1.1
.375 H. & H. Mag.	300	226	264	1.2
.44 Magnum	240	138	161	2.3
.44 Remington Mag.	240	145	169	2.2

Bullet weights are in grains.

Please note that at one end of the calibers and bullets listed, some of these rifles would be considered not powerful enough for deer. At the other end of the scale, some of them are overly powerful. Obviously, a .375 Magnum, using a 250-grain bullet at factory velocity, falls in this class. But, in some territory, where other and larger game may be encountered, some hunters might carry this particular caliber.

57—Scope Sights for Deer Rifles

In sighting in a deer rifle for maximum range and accuracy, it is best to zero in at the recommended distance. But, where this is impossible, the data provided at the 50-yard mark may be used very effectively. For example, if you sighted in a .30/06 with 180-grain bullet to hit 1.3 inches above point-of-aim at 50 yards, standard velocities, you would have an effective range coverage as follows: point-of-aim, 214 yards, and maximum range, 249 yards. Out to this distance the bullet is never more than 2.5 minutes of angles above or below point-of-aim.

Chapter 6

Shotgun Buckshot
and Slug Loads
for Deer

DEER are either taken with shotguns and buckshot, as in the South, or with a rifle, as in the North and West; and they are taken either still hunting, area watching, or by driving. These methods are in the American tradition. A combination of these methods of deer hunting, from the standpoint of firearms, is found in several of the densely settled Eastern states. Here the use of a rifle is restricted in many areas as a safety measure. Shotguns with buckshot, or shotguns with slug loads are used for *all* hunting. And for this type shooting, especially with slug loads, the smooth bore may be had with shorter barrel lengths than standard. Indeed, there are several pump action guns presently with 24-inch barrels and rifle-type open sights.

These short-barrel guns, it must be emphasized, are strictly for slug loads, and are bored straight cylinder. From the standpoint of patterns, they are not too successful in handling buckshot.

Special buckshot loads have been developed by Winchester-Western which have improved both accuracy and ranging with these multi-pellet loads. This development, very much in the previously mentioned American tradition, have a filler material around each individual buckshot, cushioning them much as buckshot has been cushioned previously by handloaders using various filler material. These filler materials range all the way from corn meal to the pouring of heated candle wax about the finished load. The best method of getting the required high pattern percentages had to await the development of polyethylene filler material and shot sleeve. Polyethylene, ground up and used to cushion the load, is utilized in the Winchester-Western Mark 5 buckshot loads.

In developing data for this chapter, I ran several hundred pattern tests with both conventional and Winchester-Western Mark 5 buckshot loads. The Mark 5 proved superior by any ballistic measurement. Loads tested in the 12 gauge were the several sizes available, 00 to 0 with a diameter of .323 going 12 to 15 to the load; size 1 special, with a diameter of .289, going 16 to the load; size 3 to 4, going 27 to the load, with a diameter of .233. In the 20 gauge, extensive testing was done with the 3 to 4 size, going 20 pellets to the standard 20-gauge 2¾-inch load.

With the 12 gauge, using all sizes in my tests and firing a series of 5 shots for each diameter pellet, I got an average of 92 per cent at 40 yards from a *full choked barrel*. Using the 3 to 4 size in the 20 gauge at the same yardage, I got an average of 93 per cent.

Dropping back to 50 yards I used the standard NRA 100-yard rifle target. With the 12 guage, using the .233 diameter pellet, going 27 to the load, I managed to put 7 pellets within the 5 ring of this target, a 12-inch circle. With the .323 diameter buckshot, going 12 to the load, I managed an average of 5 pellets within this 12-inch circle.

Several deer hunting conclusions can, I think, be drawn from all this. First, up to 50 to 60 yards these modern buckshot loads are deadly on deer. Second, they throw such extremely high pattern percentages that a well stocked gun is indicated, something especially developed for this type deer shooting. Essentially, the requirements are for a gun which throws its patterns to an exact point-of-aim, not above point-of-aim as in bird shooting. Deer are more often than not missed by over shooting, either with rifle or shotgun.

The dense patterns and potential ranging ability of these buckshot loads certainly underscore proper barrel length, gun weight, even sights, though these become of less concern as a gun is properly fitted to the individual gunner. Gun weight, it seems to me, shouldn't exceed 7 pounds, for deer hunting is fast dynamic shooting. Barrel length in a double, actually the best choice for buckshot, can well be 30 inches, if the details of weight and balance are properly met. In a pump action or auto-loader, I would recommend a barrel length of 26 inches with full choke. For the double, full and full chokes, or full and modified chokes work out nicely.

The choke best adapted to buckshot loads, incidentally, as my tests proved, is a fairly tight full constriction. Next best patterns were obtained with a modified choke. Poorest patterning with buckshot, both regular and Mark 5, was obtained with a straight cylinder barrel.

Where slug loads are used, however, a modified choke or cylinder bore delivered slightly better three-shot groups than the full choke produced. Testing slug loads was done with two types of shotguns: one a double 20-gauge Magnum, chambered for 3-inch shells; and a 12-gauge Mossberg, Model 500, pump action, with its special 24-inch straight cylinder barrel. This barrel carried open-type rifle sights.

Oddly enough, I found the 20-gauge double delivering its slugs from both barrels to a common 8-inch group at 50 yards. This gun, custom stocked to my individual specifications, had only a small front sight. This excellent accuracy is attributed to gun fit. And this accuracy certainly proved sufficient for deer shooting at all normal woods ranges.

Using the Mossberg, Model 500, pump action with its special 24-inch barrel and open sights, I managed an average group of 5 inches. Rating these guns to their exact yardage, all ballistic factors considered, I would place the range of the 20 gauge at 50 yards and that of the 12 gauge at 60 yards.

The 20-gauge Magnum double, a light pigeon gun I used for a lot of upland gunning, served a dual purpose. Blue Grouse season runs concurrently with the autumn deer season. This often puts my 20 gauge in hand, one barrel loaded with a slug load, the other with birdshot. Usually, I load the left barrel with the slug and the right with 1⅛ ounces of size 7½ shot. Then I am ready for either birds or deer. Quite often there is time to slip out the slug load and charge this barrel for grouse when birds are jumped. Quite often, too, I managed to withdraw the bird load and slip in a slug load when I have an intimation that deer are in front of me.

On two occasions, while prowling the reforested area, I downed a buck with my slug loads—ranges of about 45 to 48 yards, and they were clean kills.

With a little hunting experience the deer territory becomes an open book which is very easily read.

For out-and-out slug-load use with deer in mind, it is best to have a special gun. Remington, Ithaca, and Mossberg equip their pump-action shotguns with special short barrels and open iron sights for deer hunting. These short cylinder barrels and open sights, certainly take full advantage of the potential slug load accuracy. Tests, however, using buckshot in these open bored barrels produce too open patterns to be seriously considered for deer shooting.

Previously a 1X scope sight was available for shotguns. The particular scope had an exceptionally wide field of view. It was fast enough to even be used for some forms of wing shooting. But the ballistic fly in the ointment was the inability of the scope mount to stay on the gun without loosening, due to the heavy recoil of the smoothbore. The comparatively thin shotgun receiver gave the scope mount but little purchase, and it became loose after a few hundred rounds. Recoil in a 12 gauge, as you probably know, is much heavier than even that of a .30/06 deer rifle. So the problem of keeping a scope on a shotgun has been none too successfully met.

Recently, however, I examined a scope and mount which seems to have this particular frailty licked. This scope, a variable power, 1½ to 4X, has a very wide, clear field of view at the lower power option. After several hundred test loads it stayed on zero nicely. It would seem an excellent combination for either buckshot or slug loads. By the time this sees print, I am sure this combination, auto-loader and scope sight, will be available. It is presently being developed under the direction of I. W. Walentiny of Trade-winds, Inc.

When buckshot patterns of 93 per cent are reached at 40 yards, there can be no question of the desirability of good sights, such as this variable power scope. They are not only required for just slug loads alone. A scope sight is indicated for considerable buckshot shooting as well. Where one is confined to the use of a shotgun for deer hunting, the nearer one approaches rifle accuracy the better. Accuracy, of course, must not be obtained at the expense of dynamic gun handling qualities, nor does it need to be.

Several questions are apt to be asked in regard to slug and buckshot loads in connection with deer hunting. First, and probably the most common question is about firing slug loads in full-choked barrels: is it harmful? The answer is no. These shotgun slugs are slightly undersize, and they have fins which compress very easily in barrel passage. They may be fired from any choke. Usually, though, the best accuracy, as previously stated, is from a fairly open barrel. This, like most shotgun observations, however, is not invariably so. Some shotguns deliver very good slug-load accuracy from a fairly tight-choke constriction. Best is to test the particular shotgun you plan to use. If it has an adjustable choke, try the various constrictions, firing three-shot groups at 50 yards.

All reloading manuals have specific reloading data for slug loads, if you roll your own. My book *The American Shotgunner,* lists several slug loads, and I recommend it to your attention.

Next question often asked is about special handloads with buckshot. In reloading shotshells with buckshot, is there any merit in pouring melted candle wax about the shot charge? The benefit of such a procedure is questionable from the standpoint of improved patterns. From the standpoint of high pressures, it is not to be recommended.

Corn meal, saw dust, ground cork may be used for filler about a buckshot charge in handloads. These will produce higher patterns by several percentage points. But none of these is as effective as the use of powdered polyethylene.

The question of killing power with slug loads and buck shot is also frequently brought up. No shotgun smaller than 20 gauge is a humane handler of slugs for deer shooting. But with all three of the commonly used field guns, 20, 16, and 12 gauge, there is ample killing power at average woods ranges.

The 12-gauge slug load usually has a weight of 1 ounce. A 16-gauge slug weighs 7/8 ounce, while the 20-gauge weight for this projectile is 5/8 ounce. Translated into grains, the 12-gauge slug is 437.5 grains, the 16-gauge slug has a weight of 382 grains and the 20-gauge slug weighs 273.5 grains. All these weights are approximate and they will vary with different manufacturers.

Velocities run from around 1,330 feet for the 12 gauge, to 1,220 feet a second for the 20 gauge. Here, again, you'll find different brand factory shells producing slightly different velocities. Handloading, however, these quoted velocity figures are very close to those obtained in the respective gauges. *Killing power is ample.*

With buckshot, the killing power is excellent when deer are struck with at least 3 to 4 size .32 buckshot, or with 6 pellets of size .23. This places the maximum ranges at not more than 60 yards with all gauges and all suitable buckshot. This yardage is also maximum for slug loads. In short-range woods hunting, though, it is ample coverage. It is plenty too for a hunter on stand, with hounds doing the honors, as is often the situation in the South.

Many sportsmen believe deer hunting is at its best when a rifle is used. I question this. One has but to be on stand with hounds making music in the distance, a good shotgun in hand, properly loaded with buckshot to know a special thrill achieved in no other hunting. And where one is under the compelling necessity of using either buckshot or slug loads in a smoothbore for deer hunting, there are certain refinements of basic guns and loads which put the gunning well beyond any question of poor sportsmanship from the standpoint of humane killing. Outlined in this chapter are some of the prime requirements. The rest is a matter of knowing the quarry, woodcraft, hunting ability—all of which are taken up in succeeding chapters.

Chapter 7

The Speed of
Deer and
the Lead on
Running Targets

Ever hunt deer with a stop watch? I did. For several weeks, after the season was closed, I did my hunting with a stop watch, timing deer in sections of cover easily measured, then translating this into miles per hour. From this data it was easy to work out actual lead requirements on running game.

During this stop watch timing, I got a very good representative sampling of deer moving at a walk; a trot; a high bouncing run; and the speediest of all; a short bouncing run. While this off-season hunting with a stop watch was to measure deer speed, I was repeatedly impressed with the very pertinent hunting fact that the hunter himself has definite control over the gait of the deer he jumps still hunting, or moves on deer drives.

Moving slowly and carefully, a hunting habit deeply ingrained in me, the jumped deer responded more casually; they moved out slowly, often pausing to examine their backtrail, assessing the danger before disapppearing in the heavy cover. In the more open country, of course, they get up farther away than they do in the dense woods; but they responded in the same manner to the careful slow movement of the hunter, thus affording much greater opportunity for a humane killing shot. They would have been setup right for the most part, had I been hunting with a rifle.

Here are some typical findings on deer speed, not their top

speed, which has been clocked at around 45 miles an hour, but the speeds which are directly tied in with careful stalking, where the hunter lays it on the line in every department of woodcraft. I think they are revealing.

A forked-horn buck, slipping out through a small opening, moved 100 feet in 20 seconds. This speed clocked out at 3.4 miles an hour. A spike buck put up on a brushy ridge covered 50 feet in 5 seconds, trotting. His speed added up to 6.8 miles an hour. A doe, very typical of several for speeds, did 75 feet in 5 seconds or 10.22 miles an hour. A big three pointer, jumped on a fairly open ridge, clocked out at 17.04 miles an hour. On several occasions, after I came in close to bedded deer, surprising them close up, I got readings of 17 to 18 miles an hour; but I got no speeds higher than this. So these speeds, I believe, are representative; at least they were very consistent for the various gaits—walking, trotting, high bouncing run and low bouncing run, 55 deer clocked. Slow speeds, surely, when measured against some of the fairy tale reporting of 50 to 60 miles an hour deer speeds. But there is no cause for complacency in these seemingly slow movements of your quarry. The shot time element is short enough in all patience to underscore the need for fast precise shooting, as well as the need for lead on running game.

Some of the deer reported gave an uninterrupted 5 seconds in which to get off a telling shot. Sure, they were timed for a greater interval than this, but during their progress they were in and out of the heavy concealing cover to the extent that the longest clear interval for the shot added up to a very modest 5 seconds.

Measuring the speed of deer in typically heavy cover brings up the fair hunting question of lead on running game. Here, where many experts are constantly reporting kills at 300 to 400 yards with the game running at top speed, I suggest you make a few reservations. I have probably been in on the kill of well over a thousand deer. I haven't seen such shooting. I am not capable of doing it myself, and I think I have had as much experience in taking deer as any man. Most of those ultra long-range 300 to 400 yard shots, where the deer goes head over heels at the rifle report, are made with a good Remington portable typewriter, not a Remington rifle.

Out of the welter of my own experience hunting deer, I place the outer range limits for sure humane killing on running game at not more than 100 to 120 yards. Fifty yards is a much better and surer distance. If you are a bow hunter, see to it that the range is always within 50 yards.

These short-range requirements for humane killing of deer are no great handicap, for there is seldom any shooting much beyond 35 to 50 yards, despite all reporting to the contrary. I recall one such fanciful report of a gunner taking a running deer at 400 yards, using a .270 Winchester, a 130-grain bullet driven at a muzzle velocity of 3,100 feet a second. This deer was going all out for no good reason I could discover from reading the interesting account. For, if a hunter can put one into full flight at 400 yards, he certainly needs to sharpen his stalking ability as well as his marksmanship.

This deer, as you may suspect, presented a shooting problem of no mean proportions. It crossed a small opening of about 20 feet, the only place where the hunter could bring off the shot. So, leading him properly for 400 yards, carefully calculating his top speed of 45 miles an hour, the hunter touched off the shot. As to be expected, the game went head over heels with a broken neck.

This, of course, makes intriguing reading and no doubt reinforced the hunter in his estimation of his own prowess. Let's see. Flight time of a 130-grain bullet over 400 yards, driven at a velocity of 3,100 feet a second at the muzzle would be .5 second. A deer moving at 45 miles an hour would be covering ground at 66 feet a second, lead required, 33 feet. Obviously, this shot takes on an added virtue when you consider the very pertinent fact that the deer not only crossed the opening, but was well within the area when this paragon of a rifleman broke its neck with a well placed shot!

This rifleman, however, would be considered just an ordinary shot, when compared with another expert who reported killing a running deer at 500 yards with his trusty handgun. I set these two episodes down here as examples of the unrealistic reports which are causing many not too experienced hunters to wound game by attempting shots well beyond the capabilities of both the gun and the gunner. At the same time I make a plea for more mature and realistic writing on the subject.

A logical approach to the problem of lead on running game, tied in directly with reasonable ranges and speeds, makes a constructive contribution to your shooting. It enables you to pass up those impossible shots. It will give you due pride in making a skilled short-range kill on your running targets. Note, please, that the top speed registered in my stop watch hunting of deer is much below that which they are capable of moving. More, you'll note that these deer, with few exceptions, were moving away at an angle. So there will be shots where the average woods speed of around 18 miles an hour must be taken into consideration. There will be many more times, however, when the *apparent* speed governs the amount of lead required for a telling hit.

Apparent speed, as you know, is the speed observed from the standpoint of the hunter. The fastest deer speed checked out in my stop watch hunting was 17.04 miles an hour. This deer covered ground at 22.5 feet a second. If we take the bullet flight time over 100 yards for average woods rifles, such as those discussed in a previous chapter, we find this adds up to approximately .10 to .14 seconds. With the deer passing at right angles, where actual and apparent speed would be the same, the lead for the faster woods bullet would be 2'6", and for the slower moving bullet, such as the .30/30, 170-grain and the .35 Remington, 220-grain, the lead would be about 3'6".

You see, plainly, why shooting running deer at much over 100 yards is a gamble. By the same token, when you reduce yardage to an average 35 to 50 yards, as found in most heavy cover, leads are greatly lessened. You are not under the compelling necessity of having an aiming point beyond the game itself.

More, when apparent speed is considered, actual lead for most short-range deer shooting is reduced to a minimum. The longest lead, of course, is with the game passing at right angles to your stand. But, this is actually the rare shot. About 98 per cent of the time the deer is either approaching you while you are trail watching or area watching, or on the receiving end of a drive on the one hand, or on the other, away from you after being jumped.

Suppose you put up a deer in comparatively open cover. There is a clearing 100 feet wide, 300 feet long through which the deer moves. The game covers this 300 feet in 20 seconds, and this is not fast. In addition, he angles to the right, the width of the clearing up to 100 feet, same length of time. The rate of this angling progress is the speed you must consider in making proper lead for the shot. Twenty seconds to cover 100 feet, the apparent speed, indicates a rate of 3.4 miles an hour. At 50-yard range, the lead

The order on the trail when these two does and the big buck come out to feed is definitely ladies first. But when they return to their bedding ground after an early morning bait of apples, the buck will go first. This is something to always remember when trail watching. If your position doesn't tip off the first arriving does during an evening watch, you have a very good chance of intercepting a buck after they have passed.

with an average woods rifle having a muzzle velocity of 2,500 feet a second, would be about 3 to 4 inches.

The vital area, the target you must hit for a clean kill, is about 12 inches in diameter. This target, incidentally, is not best visualized as a 12-inch flat circle, but with the depth of a ball, comprising the chest and shoulder area of your quarry. With only a 4-inch lead requirement, the size of this vital area is sufficiently large to allow you to disregard lead entirely for such shots.

One essential of considering proper lead, is to have this unvarying target always in mind. You must make your play for the vital area of the game, regardless of the position of the animal. I'll have more to say about this in another chaper. But I feel this should be tied in directly here with the problem of lead. Deer moving at an acute angle toward or from your position, present the same problem as that encountered in shooting up or down hill. The target is foreshortened. When the game is moving away from you, the more conspicuous part of the retreating animal is the rump. All too often it becomes the aiming point under the excitement of firing. This is especially true if you have several alternatives, such as a head or neck shot, as well as the chest area which you might use for target. But, if you have psychologically conditioned yourself to take only the chest area as target, there is much less chance of being distracted by a more conspicuous part of the deer. Just remember, if you have decided on one aiming point, the vital chest area, you'll remember to angle in your shot to this target, regardless of the position of the game.

Some authorities expounding on deer shooting recommend several vital areas which you might select for the shot. But, until you have had plenty of shooting experience at running deer targets, you had better confine your efforts to the largest and most effective target, the chest area. Obviously a neck shot, when properly brought off, is excellent. So, for that matter, is a head shot. But essentially both these targets are better attempted when the deer is standing and you have a reasonable short-range shot. After plenty of experience shooting running deer, both the head shot and neck shot can be successfully brought off at short range. I have killed deer using these aiming points on several occasions. Don't, however, attempt them until you have the *feel* of your rifle from long use, and have killed a number of running deer by using the chest area as aiming point.

Just remember that the previously mentioned shooting problem, with a deer crossing an opening at an apparent speed of 3.4 miles an hour, with a required lead of only 4 inches, could very well cause you to miss a head shot, or bungle a neck shot. But the large vital area of the chest would be comparatively easy to hit. As for the spine shot, often advocated, this occurs usually when a hunter places his bullet too high and too far back.

Lead on running game differs only in detail, never principle. It is always apparent lead with which you must be concerned. Sometimes actual and apparent speed coincide, for example, when a deer passes at right angles to your stand. But more often apparent speed is much less than the actual speed, which makes lead requirement much less than usually supposed.

Once, hunting along an old logging road on an early October morning, I had this well exemplified. A rain-laden storm wind blew casually across the cover, making the multi-colored creation fresh with a wet incarnadine beauty. This storm canceled out the possibility of seeing fresh sign, but it did have compensations. The piping wind caroming through the maples nullified the sounds of my movements. There was no need to pay much attention to hunter sounds. Following the road along a hillside, watching the cover to either side, I arrived by easy slow stages at a steep gulch. Almost immediately a six-point buck broke cover across the creek.

He no doubt had watched my progress from his sheltered bed in some low growing hemlocks, undecided whether to stay put or make a break for the top of the ridge. But in studying the cover I shifted position, putting me out of sight of those keen eyes—even if not out of mind. He stepped cautiously from the concealment of those hemlocks to see what had become of me. His movement caught my eye at once. Then, knowing he had been detected, he tried for the cover at the top of the ridge. He moved at a top speed of around 18 miles an hour, running almost directly away from me. Due to the angle involved, his apparent speed was about 2 or 3 miles an hour, no more.

My rifle this day was a Model 71 Winchester .348, using a 200-grain bullet at about 2,500 feet a second muzzle velocity. The size of the vital area target in the chest area of my quarry was sufficiently large to compensate for any lead required. At the crack of the rifle the buck dropped. The bullet had expanded to about 80 calibers without blowup, had cut the two rearmost ribs, angled forward to disrupt the heart, then made exit ahead of the off shoulder.

Had this buck been running at right angles to the line of fire, lead would have been much more at this range of 100 yards. But this allowance wouldn't have been taken by selecting an aiming point ahead of the running animal. *Lead is always the amount of allowance ahead of* the vital area you intend to hit. If this buck had been moving at right angles to me at a speed of 10.22 miles per hour, at a range of 100 yards, lead would have been about 1'7" with the Model 71, .348 Winchester. This amount of allowance would have afforded an aiming point on the deer itself, the neck. To simplify this further, you must consider the built-in allowance of the 12-inch vital area you intend to hit. This, even at the expense of reiteration, is sufficiently large to compensate for lead. Actually, for a clean kill, the game passing at right angles to you at 100 yards, a very long running shot, the allowance would scarcely put your aiming point much beyond the shoulder, maybe 9 to 12 inches.

A 9- or 12-inch lead ahead of the shoulder would be quite uncertain except for the helpful factor of using some part of the deer for the aiming point. This, it seems to me, also indicates the limitations or range when shooting at running deer—a distance previously indicated as being not more than 100 to 120 yards.

In connection with those often reported long-range shots on running game, I suggest you take a pencil and paper and mark off the typical movements of a running deer. Note that your sketch is more or less a series of widely spaced N's. The game is on the ground, then it is above the ground. If it is running all out, those bounces tend to be faster, shorter. At a medium rate they are longer, higher. In either event, if you are under the compelling necessity of leading your game by any great amount, you have two movements for which you must compensate, upward and down movement, and forward movement. Either of these is sufficient to cause you to miss. Both together certainly complicate any leading where the aiming point must be off target entirely— matter of fact they complicate lead even when the aim is directly on target.

What's to be done? First examine critically your sketch of a running deer. Now, draw a straight line forward at the apex of the leaps, another at the point where the game touches the ground.

At these two points a deer hasn't any upward or downward movement with which to complicate your lead. The only motion with which you must be concerned is forward. In short, one of the two movements is eliminated. Best, if at all possible, take the shot just as the deer touches the ground, making your play for this particular position at all times, unless the cover is such that you get the best target presentation at the top of the leap.

You must, of course, know something of range estimation for proper lead evaluation, if for no other reason than to see that there is no obligation for any great amount of lead. *To simplify this range finding, it is best to reduce all ranges to short range, medium range, long range.* You may call anything under 35 yards as being short range, with medium ranges being anything from 35 to 100 yards, long range 100 to 300 yards.

The usual 1/16-inch bead on a 24-inch barreled rifle subtends about 3 inches at 50 yards, 6 inches at 100 yards, 9 inches at 150 yards, 12 inches at 200 yards. A scope post of the flat-top type covers about 4 inches at 100 yards, 6 inches at 150 yards and 8 inches at 200 yards. A Dot reticule covers about 2 inches at 100 yards, 3 inches at 150 yards, 4 inches at 200 yards, and 8 inches at 400 yards. These figures are only approximate, for the *exact* size of the bead or reticule is not known; but they are sufficiently accurate for our range-finding purpose.

Suppose, for example, I want the center of impact to be just back of the shoulder, but in order to hit this particular spot I must have about 9 to 12 inches of actual lead. I find my front sight, a 1/16-inch bead covering the essential vital area by about half—6 inches. The range, obviously, with this amount of sight coverage is 100 yards. I am not greatly concerned with the actual inches of lead required, but see it in terms of what the sight covers—deer don't wait around for any great amount of lead calculation. I swing my sight ahead of the shoulder and touch off the shot. At best I have probably 12 inches of lead, perhaps slightly more. But the size of the target compensates for slight errors of aim.

If the shot is a medium-range one of 50 yards, the bead subtends 3 inches. Lead is proportionately reduced, but it is still about the same in terms of the amount the bead subtends at the shorter distance. Your lead will not be consciously taken, but the requirements indicate that you must get out in front of the selected center of impact by a bead width or two; that is all. It should be subconscious, this leading, and it will be if it isn't complicated by impossible calculations.

Running shots are much easier in practice than in the telling. You decided this moving target requires some lead. The range may be 50 yards; it may be 55 yards; again it may be 45 yards. Don't try to be too precise. Devote your talents to selecting a good clear opening for the shot. Never take a shot at any range while the aiming point is off target. What I preach here, and practice afield, is simplification of lead requirements tied in with apparent speed of the game at short woods ranges, for the less complication there is to the lead picture, the more accurate you'll shoot and the more humane kills you make.

This, inevitably, brings up the entire problem of off-hand shooting—snapshooting if you will. For at least 98 per cent of all deer killed are taken from the standing position, *at less than 100 yards range*—all experts "punditing" about long-range deer shooting to the contrary. Let's look into the actual mechanics of snapshooting.

Chapter 8

Snapshooting

Deer

SNAPSHOOTING ties together many loose ends of your rifle shooting techniques. It pre-supposes perfect rifle fit from butt plate to muzzle. Any stocking dimension not right on your deer rifle, when measured against this fast off-hand shooting, can well cancel out your opportunity. This, of course, doesn't mean the lightest rifle procurable. Indeed, the contrary is usually indicated. For it must be remembered that fast shooting places emphasis on accuracy, not entirely target-range accuracy, but an accuracy about equally compounded of small grouping and speed. This means that your rifle must be heavy enough to have some inertia, light enough to get into action with dispatch. Achieve this and you stay on target for the brief, almost immeasurable, instant required to get off the shot.

Avoid the extra heavy rifle. Avoid the ultra light weights.

Snapshooting underscores proper sights, a subject touched upon in a previous chapter. It places special emphasis on shooting form, as you probably know. Neither precision or speed can be achieved in off-hand shooting unless perfect shooting form is part of your rifle technique.

Shooting form, however, has little in common with the target shot—just as proper stocking for snapshooting has little in common with target rifle stocking. Actually, there is a much closer relationship between off-hand rifle shooting and upland shotgunning.

Difficult assignment this snapshooting? Not really, once you dismiss a lot of claptrap masquerading as snapshooting knowhow. It's really a matter of getting down to a few easily learned, off-hand, rifle shooting techniques.

Perhaps it is best to start by pointing out what snapshooting is *not*. You'll run onto the term *half-snap* in some of the *writings* of expert "punditing" about snapshooting. This term implies that the act of snapshooting might further be divided into smaller segments, where one might achieve an *eighth-snap*. Thus the word snapshooting is made meaningless. Webster's Dictionary states, "SNAP-SHOT. A quick offhand shot, made without deliberately taking aim over the sights." Here, again, is a misleading statement to the gunner, for sights *are* used in snapshooting, but for the most part subconsciously. In snapshooting, a rifle takes on some of the attributes of a shotgun, and is pointed as well as aimed or sighted. But, none the less, sights work their magic.

There is no way of finding the best stocking for an individual's snapshooting rifle, except by shooting; and this doesn't mean orthodox target shooting, either. Duplicate a fast snapshooting, off-hand field shot where the shot is made as the rifle butt touches the shoulder, using a 12-inch bullseye at 50 yards. Do this for 5 shots, then assess your resulting group. Never mind the fact that it is a large group, much beyond the telling. See if you can find a common center for the group. If you cannot, use the same 12-inch target and fire at 25 yards—fast, a true snapshot each time. Is this common center high, low, or to either side of your aiming point? The group placement under snapshooting conditions will indicate the stocking dimension is not right.

If you consistently shoot high, the comb of the rifle is probably too high for the type sights you are using. This is a common fault when a rifle is stocked for a scope sight and is used with open ones. Shooting to the right? The comb is too thick. Shooting to the left? The comb is too thin. Low shooting pre-supposes a stock which is slightly too short, a too low comb, or both. Checking your rifle out for snapshooting should be done *after* you have carefully sighted it in at a benchrest or prone. What you are testing, snapshooting, is rifle fit to the point where some of the aiming is accomplished by gunfit.

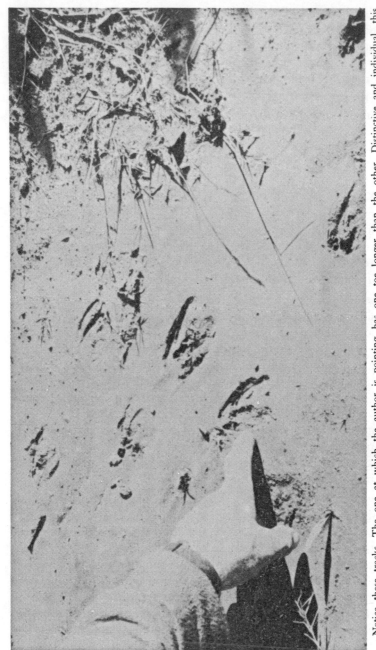

Notice these tracks. The one at which the author is pointing has one toe longer than the other. Distinctive and individual, this track could be recognized among many. Such attention to detail helps in tracking down and recovering wounded deer.

You'll note that in testing your rifle for snapshooting, you have touched upon the requirements for proper shotgun stocking, where the eye is actually used as the rear sight. With a properly fitted rifle, an aperture sight, this is actually the case. It is also true of scope sights. Even with orthodox open sights, snapshooting finds the same employment for the eye—its use as a rear sight.

You aim, surely. Yet, when the time interval is compressed for getting off the vital shot with a rifle, the routine takes on many of the attributes of shotgunning. One might say in all truth that snapshooting is compounded of about equal parts of pointing and aiming.

This pointing or aiming, if you like the term better, starts with gun mounting. Al Lyman, fern picker, trapper, woodsman and hunting partner has always contended that you aim a snapshooting deer rifle with your feet! "Get your feet 'pinted' right," Al says, "and the rest is as easy as falling off a log." Before getting the ultimate laugh from this old backwoodsman's statement, consider it a bit. Any skill, whether golfing, boxing, or gunning, starts with good foot work.

Al Lyman takes a running deer with a more effortless technique than anyone with whom I have ever hunted. I have watched him time after time on running shots, and I have never seen the game catch him off-balance. Always, as part of the snapshot, those feet of his were pointing right. Indeed, to see him cat-footing along a ridge, you knew the shot was in the making before the game came out of the concealing thicket.

Breaking this down into its component parts, it adds up to balance a light stepping which leaves those all important feet close to shooting position at all times. Consider the following a moment, rifle in hand. A deer is passing from right to left in the foreground. If your left foot is stepped slightly forward when the game jumped and you know its direction of travel, you can swivel at the hips as the rifle comes effortlessly to your shoulder. You have complete coverage of the escape route.

Suppose, though, that left foot is pointed slightly to the right of the spot where the game appeared. It takes the same course. You turn, but before the target is in the clear for the shot, you are in a very cramped position. Your only alternative now is to shift position and move those feet to get your quarry under the sights. Try that with your rifle at your shoulder. It's extremely awkward, all of which brings us back to Al Lyman's original contention that good snapshooting starts with good foot work—aiming with one's feet.

While you have that unloaded rifle in hand; and I assume you have checked it as you should to determine that it *is* unloaded, try the routine again. This time scrape your left foot back slightly, while turning to the left on the ball of your right foot—all the while you are bringing up the rifle. Note that you have made a left face, giving you an easy position to .cover *all* the territory through which the bouncing deer is moving.

This same routine would put you on target if the deer passed from left front to right, except now you would scrape your right foot back slightly while turning on the ball of your left foot. This, of course, assumes that you shoot from the right shoulder. If you shoot from the left shoulder, then the procedure in each instance would be just the opposite.

This aiming with the feet, as Al Lyman called it, gives you one other advantage. While the rifle is temporarily subordinated to foot work, it is still very much in the picture. For while it is coming to taw, so to speak, it should be pointed directly at the game from first to last. It is ready aimed even as the butt touches the shoulder. There is now no necessity for checking the sights for they are on target beyond any improvement. If they are not, then either your gun mounting and foot work or rifle stocking should come under the gravest suspicion.

In testing this particular contention, as I hope you'll test *all statements* made in this *Deer Hunter's Guide,* try some dry firing. Bring your rifle to your shoulder from the carry, and at the instant the butt touches your shoulder, get off the simulated shot. You'll notice that if there is no delay, no trying for a more accurate sight picture, you were on target for the instant required to fire.

Probably the most unusual factor of this type shooting, and I am sure you have noticed it in mounting your rifle, is that your eyes never once leave the target. Sights are always subordinate. When the sights intrude to the point where the target is subordinate, the shot is fired from memory. You cannot focus your eyes on the target and sights at the same time, nor is it necessary. In driving a nail with a hammer, you do not look at the hammer. Your attention is on the nail you plan to hit. If you want a smashed thumb, let your attention wonder to the hammer for an instant. While the analogy is not exact, and you end up with nothing more than a miss with a rifle when your attention is distracted from the target, it connot be too strongly recommended that you keep your eye on the target, first, last and all the time.

Snapshooting with accuracy and dispatch starts with correct rifle carry. Watch any experienced woodsman when he is momentarily expecting a shot and you see this examplified. There are three very essential methods of carrying a rifle. First, and probably best for the average hunter, is to carry the rifle at the balance in the left hand, if he shoots from the right shoulder.

Assuming you are carrying your rifle in this manner and deer is put up. You instinctively point the gun at him, even as it is brought to your shoulder. In bringing the rifle into firing position, it is presented with the left hand sweeping it up, always more or less level, to shoulder height. The right hand reaches for the trigger guard and pistol grip, instinctively cocking it or releasing the safety. The rifle actually comes up ready aimed.

As you can see, proper rifle fit is very essential.

When your left hand presents the rifle for the shot from this carry, you are turning, getting into position, with no time lost. All this while the muzzle of the gun is pointing at the target. Now, with the rifle at your shoulder, you should find it extremely hard not to be looking directly at the target through the sights. Sound complicated? Try it on target—a 12-inch circle representing the vital area of a deer, 50-yard range. In reality, if you attend to each factor of the routine, you'll marvel at the simplicity of achieving snapshooting speed and accuracy.

I like this left hand carry. (It would be a right hand carry if you shot from the left shoulder.) It enables me to ease brush out of my way, part the fern with my right hand and move with due caution on a deer trail. And the rifle is always easily presented for the shot.

Another carry which I often use in comparatively open cover has the rifle slung from my left shoulder, muzzle down, trigger guard and forearm to the front. In going into action from this carry, the rifle is given a half turn counter clockwise, ending with the muzzle pointing at the quarry. Then the mounting is very much that of the left hand carry, with the rifle presented to the right hand in the same fashion.

The third method of carry, often called the Indian carry, is with the rifle cradled in the two arms, muzzle to the left. This carry has plenty of merit from the standpoint of both speed and comfort. You'll have the right hand at the grip of the rifle, thumb on safety or hammer, the left hand over the right.

To go into action from this carry, the left hand slides forward as the rifle is brought to the shoulder; that's all. Here, as with the two other positions described, first aiming, or pointing out, is achieved as the primary step of making a snapshot. This first aiming is essential under all circumstances. It starts with the feet, just as Al Lyman says; it is complemented by the barrel of the rifle as it is brought up, finishing with the sights all lined up for the shot.

Essentially, snapshooting is primarily the utilization to best advantage of the limited time a hunter has in which to get off the shot. It is just as much a requirement for the off-hand shooting of standing deer as it is for one that is moving. It is always good rifleman-woodcraft to assume any standing deer poses the threat of immediate and violent movement. *Snapshooting, however, is not a hasty, ill-considered shot at brush movement or poorly defined target. Such shooting is criminally stupid under all circumstances.*

Snapshooting requires practice, plenty of off-season practice with your deer rifle. In this practice, the full routine of readying the rifle for the shot and simulating the shot by pulling the trigger is only part of requirements. Continue by a simulated reloading. This evenly spreads the emphasis over the entire routine. You'll find that with practice that the reloading become subconscious, just as most of the readying the rifle for the shot and aiming is subconscious. You'll not be caught with an empty rifle when you are required to snap in a fast second shot for a clean kill.

All this practice should be clean-cut, smooth, precise, fast. After acquiring skill in this method of gun mounting, of getting off the shot with dispatch, you'll make the habit of speed a requirement for *all* your shooting, even from a sitting position for a long-range shot. The first aim, you'll discover, is always your best aim.

Longer range deer shots are seldom taken offhand, of course. They are your sitting, kneeling, sometimes prone shots. Quite often you'll use a tree to steady your hand as a shot *is* taken from the standing position. But your snapshooting training comes in very handy here. You'll make those shots fast, no waiting around, unless it is for the game to get into a better position for a telling hit. This long-range shooting, as previously pointed out, is a very small segment of all deer shooting. Snapshooting at short woods ranges is what puts venison on the table.

A skilled woodsman may owe much of his reputation as a deadly game shot to the fact that he has plenty of stalking ability. But in addition to this stalking skill, rest assured he is a capable snapshot. Extended experience has taught him that no rifle shot at game, however easy, calls for less than top skill. He never lapses from this high standard of snapshooting skill under any circumstances. Just remember that the entire problem of deer hunting is one of related skills. Shooting cannot be divorced from woodcraft, and woodcraft without shooting skill is useless.

Chapter 9

Trail Watching
Is a
Fine Art

THE fine art of deer-trail watching is something the average hunter takes all too lightly. He often approaches trail watching as something of much less worth than either still hunting or driving, a fill in. But, in all probability, deer trail watching is the most successful method of hunting which can be employed by   lone individual. It takes a high degree of hunting skill, too.

Once discussing deer trail watching with a knowledgeable Indian hunting friend, he made a remark which I have always remembered and have applied to my own trail watching. *"The less you move,"* he said, *"the more you see."*

We were dressing out a beautiful five-point buck, one of eight deer which had come under our observation while we were sheltered by the upthrust roots of a windfall. The deer trail we watched snaked into an oak grove where the acorns lay thick upon the ground.

We were posted there for five solid hours, waiting, watching, hours which had at times dragged by on leaden feet, at other times tiptoed with suspense as deer approached. No casual undertaking this trail watching as exemplified by my Indian friend. I was impressed by the thought he gave to the selection of just the proper position, both from the standpoint of shelter and territory coverage.

We naturally had the choice of several positions. But the place he selected for our watching underscored several prime factors of successful trail watching. It had good wind coverage, something which will be treated more fully in the next chapter. It was selected for comfort, for after all we expected to be in position for several hours.

A steady rain had shaped our hunting during the morning, keeping us well down slope on deer trails. It now pinpointed our best stand for trail watching. For during this cold rain, the thermal drag of wind set downhill, down draw, and down valley, away from the higher ground.

This naturally placed us below the feeding area we watched. Our stand was below three distinct deer trails leading out of sheltering cover farther along the slope. A deer moving along these trails, sensitive nose to wind, had complete news coverage of what took place in the oak grove feeding area. He would know not only how many deer had moved along these trails previously, but how many were presently eating acorns in the grove. Any suggestion of hunter scent would be carried to him from the high ridges, if you posted there.

Change the wind and the trail activity changed. These deer trails, favored today because of the storm, would be abandoned for those coming along the top of the ridge if the thermal drift of wind was up-slope. While our position down-slope didn't give us complete coverage of the entire feeding area, it did put us one up on all trails the present thermal drag of wind indicated the deer would use. We waited. And this waiting is an art seldom learned by the casual once-a-year deer hunter. Indeed, it is seldom he realizes, as you do, that trail watching is a very exacting art.

Try sitting in just an ordinary chair, not moving for an hour, two hours, four hours. Check all the little involuntary movements you make—shifting position, coughing, lighting a smoke. After this experiment you'll probably question the ability of even the most lazy Indian and equally lazy woodsman, such as my Indian friend and myself to remain quiet for any great length of time. But it can be done.

First, and of primary importance in remaining comparatively quiet, is to make yourself a comfortable place to sit—one where you may lean back, have a headrest against a tree stump or a slab of bark placed behind you for that purpose. Select a position where you may occasionally shift your legs, slowly, carefully.

Typical, northern, heavy cover where deer ranges are reduced to a scant 33-50 yards, and it must be a snapshot.

Gather dry leaves and forest duff from under sheltering trees and make yourself a comfortable seat.

It is all important for you to be so comfortable you have little necessity for moving about to relieve cramped muscles, which cause cold feet. But what little movement you *do* make must have some shielding from your quarry. For, remember, a deer will have *your* position under observation *before* you have him under your sights. A trophy buck never commits himself to any opening until he has conned all possibilities from the screening brush. You can easily cancel out your chance for a shot by movement, without suspecting game was in your vicinity.

You can take a profitable leaf from the notebook of a duck-hunter, making a blind for your trail watching, but with one noted exception. A duck hunter may stand up abruptly for the shot. This you cannot do when trail watching for deer. Here, you must be the soul of caution. Your foreground blinding on a deer-trail watching stand must never interfere with a slow, snail-slow, make-ready for the shot. For this often means the difference between an easy shot at a comparatively slow moving deer or a shot at one moving out at an alerted run.

A neutral-colored tarp draped over a few bushes is excellent blinding, provided it is so placed that there is a minimum movement for either observation or shooting. Better yet is a light screening of brush which enables you to see through it, but still breaks up your body outline. Such brush screening is very effective in breaking up indications of those small movements incurred in trail watching.

When I say small and cautious, too much emphasis cannot be placed on these. Primarily you have located your stand to give effective coverage of the deer trails you watch or the feeding area under observation. You have selected a comfortable position which you can maintain without undue shifting about. Movement makes *all* wildlife suspicious. Indeed, a trained woodsman pinpoints movement at once. Any screening which helps to cancel out those small, cautious movements is all to the good. Be cautious in bringing up your binoculars for a detailed look at some suspicious shadow; don't move your head abruptly.

In trail watching, you'll be alerted time after time by the un-natural swaying of a fern, the slight movement of a huckleberry bush. These small movements instantly rivet your attention on that particular area until the disturbance resolves itself. Most often such movement is created by a bird or a leaf ticking down through the flame-colored autumn woods, but not always. Such small movement in many cases is also your first intimation of deer. Remain still. Watch. Always remember that, insofar as deer are concerned, the closer you approach immobility, the closer you are to total invisibility.

This particular contention will be exemplified time after time in your trail watching. A deer may detect a stray ravel of hunting scent, catch you in some small overt movement. At once those large ears are flipped forward as he listens. His eyes will be watching for that movement to be repeated. If you remain perfectly still you remain, in effect, invisible to the game. He has yet to identify the noise and movement, and until he does, he will watch an appreciable length of time before dismissing the occurrence as of no importance.

Quite often you'll witness a performance of stamping and blowing as the deer tries to drum up a bit more movement for identifying purposes. It is the same with sound, other than those normally associated with the game itself. Sound touches off the alarm, putting the deer on the alert, that is arresting sound, sound with no identifying movement.

Once, trail watching during a late afternoon, I saw a beautiful six-point buck angling down a trail, feeding casually on black huckleberry brush. This day I had elk in mind for the deer season had but recently closed, and I expected a herd of elk to use this trail before nightfall. I watched this regal buck with just as much interest, however, as if the season were open.

To see what his reaction would be to noise, I reached down and secured a small limb when he was fully occupied with his feeding and wouldn't detect the movement. When his head went down behind the dense huckleberry brush again, I threw the limb well beyond him, as he was only about thirty feet away from me. Instantly, that proud head came up, the cedar-stained antlers agleam in the late evening light. The limb hit a small hemlock then ticked down through the brush. He studied the disturbance for an instant, evaluated it, then returned to his feeding.

I picked up and broke a small twig. The buck turned, gave this sound his attention. I waited, unmoving, for perhaps five minutes while he tested wind, watched and listened. When he resumed feeding, I broke the twig again, giving it a sharp snap. Again his head came up. He took a cautious step down-trail in my direction. Then he resumed his feeding.

What baffled him was sound quite acceptable to him as it was of a type made by the game itself, but there was no associated movement, no identifying source. After a third snapping of the twig, he came on down the trail, his nose on the crosswind, huge ears funneled forward to receive any sound. In this manner, he came within twelve feet of my stand before a stray ravel of hunter scent touched him off. Then he went bounding along the slope, snorting indignantly.

This stand I occupied would, seemingly, violate some of the suggestions made about proper posting for deer trail watching. I had no screening of brush, only background coverage, with a large fir to break up my outline. I was dependent to a great degree on complete immobility for concealment. The post was selected because the thermal wind, still uphill at the time I saw the buck, was due for a late evening change before those elk traveled the trail out to their opening feeding area in a logging slash. But even with the thermal wind uphill the cross haul carried my scent away from the trail, an almost ideal setup.

My rifle was directly in front of me, placed on two forked sticks sharpened and shoved into the ground for the purpose. These sticks were high enough so my gun could be picked up slowly, with a minimum of movement. This rifle placement is a requisite of proper trail watching under all circumstances, ready at all times, and capable of being brought into action with a minimum of movement.

One cannot hold a rifle in hand indefinitely, trail watching, nor a bow and arrow, either. So this particular pre-readying of your arm, whatever its nature, is something for serious study. I suggest that archers trail watching for deer might spend a very profitable period experimenting before the hunt on this bow placement. What is the best position so that the weapon might be brought to bear with the least movement? With a rifle, assuming you are sitting on post, this is best achieved with two forked sticks shoved into the ground. This, in effect, cancels out several movements *before* you are under the compelling necessity of going into action. With a bow and arrow the requirements are essentially the same.

I have worked this out with a rifle, but I confess that I haven't taken the problem apart from the standpoint of getting a bow and arrow readied for the shot. Obviously, though, the bow should be standing well up, with the arrow lying almost nocked, or perhaps nocked, pointing in the direction of the expected shot.

Archers of an inventive turn of mind might even contrive a monapod which would telescope to be carried in an arrow quiver. This could be extended and thrust into the ground to hold the bow and arrow readied for a quick draw.

This problem of getting into action with a minimum of movement brings us directly back to that light screening of brush. If you are using such blinding, see that it is placed far enough away from you so it will not interfere with the swinging of the gun to the right or left to cover all possible angles from which you might get a shot. With more experience, a bit more self-discipline, you'll find that sitting in front of a dense screening of brush is just about as effective as sitting behind it. Your outline is effectively broken up, and as long as you remain perfectly still, you are invisible to the game. This takes plenty of self-discipline. It touches upon the previously mentioned necessity of having a very comfortable position in which you can achieve, and maintain, complete immobility.

Deer trail watching falls into two classifications. First is of the type most of this writing has touched upon, the more common kind, watching trails leading from one security cover to another, trails leading to and from feeding areas. The other type is area watching, directly where the feeding occurs. The latter is very effective under some circumstances, whereas at other times it is scarcely worth your while.

Frequently, deer move out to some favored feeding spot in heavily hunted territory timing their arrival with total darkness. You may find an old abandoned orchard or cultivated area littered with tracks. But all your late evening and early morning watching will fail to disclose any game. Solution to this hunting problem? Scout those trails they are using in their comings and goings. Follow them well into the protective cover where the deer are day bedding.

Quite often you will find these deer moving as much as a half mile to get to some exposed feeding area, timing their arrival to coincide with first darkness. But, those deer are up and traveling well before darkness. Quite often you have as much as a full hour of good light on the trail they are using. All you need to do to get this game under your gun is select a stand much closer to their day bedding area.

By careful scouting you can pinpoint their well used trails, finding a good spot for your trail watching where you can intercept them in good shooting light. Experienced woodsmen know these alternatives to watching a feeding area in heavily hunted territory. They take full advantage of the knowledge.

One might even consider a distinct type of trail watching as a third classification, though actually it isn't, for you will be watching almost the same type trails as the game use between feeding and bedding areas. This is an early morning to late evening trail watching in heavily hunted territory, the heavier hunted the better from the standpoint of effective trail watching. In this type trail watching, you pay due regard to natural escape routes, trails between densely grown sections of territory where deer normally lay up for the day. The movements of other hunters thrashing about in the brush are constantly pushing deer out of the security cover, sending them along the normal escape routes toward other places where they might find security—swamps, densely grown bits of upland cover.

With just a bit of study, all this game movement can be turned to your trail-watching advantage. Select a spot which drains off a lot of average hunting territory. Bypass the easily accessible fringe areas. These will be covered by the average hunter on the prowl. Get up to those ridges and densely wooded hills beyond this. Find a well used deer trail, then stay put. Here, in effect, you are on the receiving end of a gigantic deer drive, with *all* those prowling hunters making a potential contribution to your success.

Come prepared to stay the full day. Bring a lunch, a thermos bottle of coffee; and, above all, dress for a day of inactivity in severe weather. On such an all-day stand, there will be occasions when you'll walk about briefly—cautiously, to restore circulation. But the prime consideration is a comfortable sitting position, one which you can maintain for several hours. It's like my Indian friends said, "The less you move, the more you see." That's trail watching in a nutshell.

Notice especially the ears of these deer. The doe has her ears funneled forward. The buck has his turned back. There is no direction you might approach without the sound of your movement tipping them off.

Chapter 10

Deer Trails —
Game Highways
of the Wilderness

W E HAD about two hours of good shooting light before us, then darkness. More to the point, we had about three quarters of a mile of good deer territory between us and my Jeep. All this was plenty of incentive for us to stop our cooperative still-hunting driving which Elzie Randolph and I were doing in the heavily brushed hills. Deer? We moved at least twenty bucks, does, and fawns, but none upon which we wished to place a tag, the season being still young with plenty of time to try for a trophy buck. Now, with autumn evening nipping at our heels, we had a very good part of the day to work the deer trails *outward* toward the feeding areas.

We would trail hunt, not casually, but with full knowledge of their use by the game. All deer territory is covered with a network of these well planned wilderness routes. Deer activity of any nature is tied in directly with these woodland highways. Migratory deer routes of the big Western Mule Deer are used year after year, until ultimately these trails are cut down into the flinty soil by seasonal use. Sometimes these western deer move as much as a hundred miles between summer and winter ranges. Always, however, they use the same routes.

In non-migratory deer territory, such as the Whitetail and west coast Columbia Blacktail areas, there is a crisscross of these wood-land highways.

Deer activity become much easier to anticipate once you under-stand the nature, not only of deer migratory routes, but those used almost the year around by non-migratory deer. Breaking trail activity into the obvious subdivisions we find trails are as fol-lows; escape routes, feeder trails, and pathways from one section of cover to another—all tied together to constitute the network. Sometimes you'll find one trail serving two purposes. Indeed, this is quite common practice in some type deer territory.

Trails leading into dense security bedding spots have escape routes attached. Entrance trails to such spots may be a diversity of small, scarcely defined trails. Beyond these bedding spots the threads of these smaller trails usually come together into one or two larger game trails.

Wind changes and prevailing air currents shape these trails. They also touch upon an easily read pattern of deer use. The inflow of game in late morning is always from the direction of the more open feeding areas. In late evening it is just the opposite, with the deer traffic being toward the more open country where most feed is found.

When Elzie Randolph and I started our still hunting toward my Jeep, we separated and took direction along two ridges about a hundred fifty yards apart. We didn't expect to find deer trails leading directly along the top of the ridges, entirely, but we did expect to find those pathways paralleling the ridges.

We moved at all times on those all important deer trails. In doing so we matched the direction those deer would normally move, at a time of day when they expected to hear the noises of others on those trails. Results? Elzie Randolph put up eight deer, all within easy shooting distance. I had eleven head within 50 yards of me. None of this game moved out fast. None touched off the alarm to more than a small segment of territory. All waited around, watching, listening, until we came within identifiable distance. The heavier the cover the closer we came to the game before they moved out.

My hunting partner tagged a big three-point buck (six pointer, eastern count). After the shot I angled across to him, directed by an occasional blowing on a empty cartridge, our signal for a kill.

The kill, of course, ended our hunting. But the technique of tying in hunter movement to expected game activity has scarcely any field limitations.

I have yet to spend a day on deer trails without seeing game, anywhere from three to as many as fifteen head of deer. Hunting directly tied in with an intimate knowledge of deer trails makes it easy to take deer on bare ground or snow. Game trails are always a primary consideration whether you still hunt, drive a section of territory, or just trail watch. It works equally well in Wisconsin woods, upper Michigan, or Maine. In the Modoc Forest of northern California, I sat for three days and watched the migration of Western Mule Deer. Always they held to the same series of trails, and always they would have presented easy shooting. If all this sounds like a hunter's pipe dream, I only ask that you bear with me for a few short chapters while we explore all implications of these woodland highways. For I'll return to a consideration of deer trails time after time when you and I are examining the best methods of driving big game cover, just as we did in the chapter on trail watching.

Let's examine a typical bedding ground, the trails leading into it, the escape trails leading away to other security cover. Obviously, the grounds where deer bed, the particular location, have several factors which contribute to their selection. First, and perhaps most important, is concealment. Second is shelter from storm. Third is wind coverage of the trails. Fourth is a good escape route between this bedding and other dense, sheltering cover.

Examine these day bedding requirements in detail, matching them against their respective woodland requirements, and you acquire the ability to place your finger on favored spots where deer concentrate after their foraging. Such woodland knowledge places you one up, when it comes to putting venison on the camp game rack. In many ways it gives new meaning to your hunting. You are taking it out of the luck category and substituting good basic hunting knowledge, something which always makes any hunt more interesting from start to finish.

Once, while hunting with Al Lyman, we came into a section of territory which neither of us had previously hunted. We were exploring as much as hunting. We loitered on a hill where a gaunt, silver, weathered, dead tree stood against the green reforesting. Here with much of the territory spread before us, we assessed possibilities against the time when we would return to give the area a thorough hunting.

Al Lyman pointed to a green-clad slope beyond our observatory. "See that dense jungle of hardhack, mountain willow, and cedar?" I looked in the direction he pointed. About four acres in extent, the dense growing brush lay about halfway up a long gentle rise of ground. Beyond this the woods thinned out into a representative covering of firs perhaps thirty feet tall. Then beyond this mantle of fir there was another dense growing mantle of gold and green hardhack, mountain willow, maple, and hemlock. "There," Al continued, "is where we'll find our buck."

His statement needed no answer. We had found evidence of big deer in this section all during our prospecting trip, huge tracks in the moist earth. There were bushes broken and torn where a buck had worked off a bit of his autumn aggressiveness. Prime deer hunting territory, with food, shelter and plenty of concealment. We marked it down for future hunting reference. This reforesting covered thousands of acres, but not once from the time we entered it had we been under the compelling necessity of getting away from travel on those all important game trails. Always, no matter the turning, we found trails outlining the route.

At times these led through bedding grounds where deer love to loaf after evening and morning feeding. At times they snaked across the hills from one section of territory to another. But always they were logical routes of travel, escape or security cover trails.

The larger trails, running from one section of cover to another, were well defined, easily followed. The feeder trails in the more open sections were not so well marked where the deer scattered during their morning and evening feeding periods. The dense security cover always had several trails leading into it and it always had several leading away toward other dense sections of cover. But beyond the security cover, and approaching it, these several trails were caught up into two or three main game trails.

When Al Lyman pointed out the large security cover on the slope opposite our observation point, he also pinpointed the escape route beyond this, leading to the next security cover. It added up to just the type of cover where we had taken big trophy bucks in the past.

It would be nice to go on and tell you we predicted a hunt on Al's observation and brought down a nice buck, but we didn't. Exploring this wilderness section, we had jumped eighteen deer—bucks, does, and fawns. But we came into the best section too late to actually hunt it. Turning away, we skirted the reforesting to get back to my Jeep parked on an old logging road, arriving just after dark.

Later, alone, I worked out this section, getting a big five pointer while still hunting. He fell in the first section of security cover Al Lyman pointed out from that hill.

Consider a wise old buck bedded on a sun-warmed hardhack ridge. He could have come into this bedding area from any direction. What motivated him, trailwise? Deer are creatures of habit. They never make a move, however, without some very good reason. Those deer trails have a scent pattern from previous use. Nose to ground, a deer can tell if any other deer have moved recently over this route, and, if so, the direction it or they moved. More, he can tell just about how many deer are bedding in a particular section. He knows whether anything has disturbed the bedding grounds toward which he is approaching. It is much more logical, and from the standpoint of security, more telling for deer to stay on trail than off.

The scent pattern to a great extent defines these trails. But to some extent the contour of the land also shapes them. Good wind coverage on these trails is a primary consideration to the game, something which will be more fully covered in the next chapter. Where one, two, or a half-dozen deer finish feeding and move to their security bedding to lay up for the day or to ride out a storm, the scent pattern is the foundation of safety. Other deer seeking places to bed for the day will use this cover by preference. The rich pungent odor, at times so strong it is easily detected by hunters, reassures them that the bedding area is well used and, therefore, the deer are undisturbed.

If you pinpoint a buck bedding on a certain hardhack ridge, he will be using that same bedding area a week from now, unless the rut is on, storms push him into more sheltered territory, or heavy hunting pressure moves him.

When danger threatens he is not going to panic and move out through some obvious opening just because it affords a good place for a posted hunter to shoot. No, his sneak will be along a well defined game trail leading to other security cover. This is why you can predict deer movement under all hunting circumstances.

Knowing deer trails and their use, you have little trouble in hunting unfamiliar territory. Starting with the more open feeding areas, where you'll find a crisscross of tracks in snow or on wet ground, you can follow these out, unraveling them toward the heavier brushed territory, until eventually you find them converging on a woodland highway, a main deer trail.

I recall hunting a logging slash one autumn morning. This entire area was lush with browse—huckleberry, wild vetch, salal brush, and wild clover. But there was no security cover save along the north side of this extensive logging. Here a mantle of second growth afforded prime shelter for the deer using the logging slash.

I hoped to catch my game directly on the feeding ground just after morning shooting light, but in this I was disappointed. A full moon, setting just before dawn, was incentive enough for those deer to night feed and leave the opening before daylight, that is all save a doe and two fawns which I detected slipping out toward the timber. I watched them through my binoculars. After waiting about twenty minutes, I took up their trail, knowing it would lead me toward a bedding ground.

I had scarcely entered the woods when I put up a buck. He slipped out from under a clump of huckleberry brush and vine maple, trotting away through the fern, with just his head and part of his neck showing. I snapped my rifle to my shoulder and at the report he went head over heels with a broken neck, my only aiming point.

I paced the distance back to the opening along that deer trail. He had moved into heavy cover only 35 yards before bedding. The doe and two fawns were bedding about 20 yards beyond him, going out when the buck touched off the alarm. He actually got up about 18 feet in front of where I stood on the trail, all to a pattern I have seen repeated time after time.

All deer normally move on these trails. This is the place where *they* expect to see movement and to hear noise. The slight swaying of a bush on trail is not alarming, but it touches off the alert if it is made off-trail by a hunter. It is the same way with noise: on-trail it is in place, off-trail it is not. Your hunt must be predicted on this very basic consideration to be consistently successful.

Consider the previously mentioned buck bedded on the hard-hack ridge. He hears noise on the trail he recently used to approach this area. He listens. There is the soft swish as of a tawny hide pressing back the fern or other low growing stuff, a sound he has heard innumerable times as other deer approach the bedding grounds. There is the casual snap of an occasional twig, again a very familiar sound. He regards the sound of whatever is approaching as that of an unalarmed deer. He'll wait around until the author of those sounds is in good sight—often within a few very short yards of him.

Time after time, duplicating the expected noise on deer trails, I have come within six or eight feet of deer! Once, while hunting during a storm, I crawled along a security trail, the brush so dense I couldn't stand up. I got within 8 feet of a bedded three pointer and killed him from the prone position with a light Mannlicher stocked 6.5mm.

You may take it for granted that deer always hear you. Those keen ears of theirs pick up every sound. By the same token, you may take it for granted that there is no such thing as a noiseless approach. Not even Daniel Boone himself or the great Uncas quite brought off this ideal of the storybook Indians. The game itself isn't noiseless. Neither is the hunter. It is not important, this disturbance, unless it is hunter noise and hunter movement, which is so easily identified by the game.

What is hunter movement? What is hunter disturbance? Hunter movement, so easily identified by deer, is any movement off-trail. It is usually much faster paced than that of undisturbed game; it is directly across cover, without any regard for trails—loud and persistent. This disturbance has no counterpart in the wilderness. It is directly associated with hunters, so avoid this disturbance, this consequent noise, and you are well down the trail toward successful deer hunting.

Even at the expense of reiteration, your approach to deer hunting, both literally and figuratively, is to duplicate in your movements both the sound and pace of the deer.

Chapter 11

Know
Your
Winds

ONE OF the least understood phases of all deer hunting is wind, wind in all its manifestations—thermal winds, prevailing winds, storm winds. Yet a successful deer hunter must feel the pulse of the wind at all times, lest he tip off the game. You have probably heard that all deer hunting should be done into the wind. This is over-simplification of a rather complicated problem. Actually, you tie *all* hunting to *deer habit,* which is greatly controlled by the wind.

A classic example of wind tripping up a deer drive used to occur on one of our deer stands. At times this posting proved deadly. At other times deer avoided it like the plague. When it worked, a hunter posted here had a good chance of getting some close-range shooting at a fine buck. Several nice heads were collected here.

Vagrant wind drift was suspected when the posting didn't pay off, even though there was no apparent air current one way or another. But, when I am inclined to grow careless about wind drift, I visualize this deer stand. I see the fresh deer tracks in the damp forest duff turning aside before the game crossed the small swale we posted, all this time after time.

Kills made on this stand when the deer came directly through should have tipped us off. These were always made when we put on the drive just after good shooting light in the morning. Later

100

in the day, in good weather, the stand always proved unproductive. It produced, however, on overcast days. It was excellent when a storm growled across the cover, or weather change indicated an approaching storm.

The stand itself met *all* apparent requirements for a good posting. It was directly between two good sections of security cover where deer day bed. It had a complement of deer trails leading toward it from the more open feeding areas. The game trail we posted angled around a ridge, snaked across a fairly open draw, then held its elevation across a slope toward dense third-growth security cover.

The hunter took position fairly well down the slope from the ridge marked with the deer trail. When an early morning drive was made here, with the thermal wind drift still down slope, all was well and good. During overcast days, approaching storm, or stormy weather, the set of the current was down slope. Again, the stand always produced under these circumstances. But under stable weather conditions, during mid-day, the deer weren't interested in our posting.

I might add the clarifying detail that the deer moved during a drive came from adjacent territory, or the feeding area, and made for the third-growth security cover beyond our posting. With the up-draft of wind along the ridges, those deer *had* to take some of the secondary trails to keep the security cover under their noses, so to speak. This was a matter of leaving the main trail as soon as it looped around the slope, and take a secondary trail around the ridge from the posting. Travel here not only put the deer one up on the bedding area, he got a snout full of hunter scent, pinpointing the posted rifleman.

The problem of posting this particular stand held no great difficulties once the thermal winds were given attention. With the hunter taking up a stand higher on the ridge and further around the slope on those days when the set of the thermal was up-slope, deer could move on those secondary trails with a crosswind directly to it, without the hunter coming under suspicion.

Thermal wind drift can be very deceptive at times. Wind may move so slowly you'll swear there is no air current at all. First, though, let's get our definition straight. A thermal wind, as its name implies, is an air current set in motion by temperature changes. As the temperature changes, the direction of the thermal

Snapshooting is a short-range proposition. It places emphasis on the off-hand position and a light and easily pointed rifle.

drag changes. Under stable weather conditions the trend of these thermals is down slope, down creeks and down valleys from late evening until fairly early morning. From late morning until the evening reversal, the trend of the thermal air current is up slope, up the valleys and draws, always from the lower to the higher ground.

Clearing weather after a storm sends them uphill. A storm approaching, or one in progress, sends them cascading from the higher to the lower ground.

In flat land, a lake, large pond, swamp, or forest fronting on open country acts the same as low ground in hilly territory. The set of the thermals will be *out* from the forest toward the open country, the swamp, lake or pond during late evening, until early morning. In late morning, holding all during the day under stable weather conditions, the trend of the air current will be *in* from the open country, the lake or pond.

Obviously, if you arrived at such cover during mid-morning and still hunted from the openings in toward the forest center, the thermal wind drift is against you. But, with the same still hunt in mind, starting at good morning shooting light, you would be right for the hunt, with the thermal still moving *out* from the forest toward the more open country. When the morning thermal change came, you would be on the high ground or the forest center, still in step with the thermal.

Driving deer without taking the thermal wind drifts into consideration is a very profitless undertaking. The word driving, as a matter of plain hunting fact, is a very poor descriptive term. Deer are not driven; they are moved. Put up, the game selects the escape route, moving toward other security cover. And be sure he'll have a thermal wind drift across his escape route, telling him what security or menace he is approaching.

Sometimes these thermal winds are so mild that the drift is scarcely perceptible. But it is always there, either working for or against the hunter. Sit down for any length of time, trail watching, area watching or on stand. If a deer approaches at once he may have to come within 50 yards of you from down wind before the slow moving thermal tips him off to your presence. But as you lengthen your wait, this distance is increased by the thermal drift until this 50 yards is as much as 250—either up slope or down slope, depending on the time of day you are watching.

Best hunting procedure, of course, is to take it for granted you always have a thermal wind drift under stable weather conditions. Then you can select your stand, or make your drive, or still hunt, with this in mind. Just remember that there are no exceptions to these thermals when the weather is right.

Under stable weather conditions deer normally bed on slightly higher ground, or well away from the open feeding areas. This bedding may be as much as a half mile from some favored browsing area. During the time they are moving out to feed in late evening, they have good wind coverage on the trails and on the feeding area they are approaching. If heavy hunting pressure brings them into the feeding area after dark, and after the thermal shift of wind in late evening, they'll take advantage of the day thermal to come nose-to-wind along the trails leading to the feeding. Then they will wait around until after dark and the thermal change before entering the openings. Here, so strong is the habit of traveling nose-to-wind, they will usually circle the feeding area to get the wind drift in their favor before venturing into the opening.

Returning to their bedding area next morning, with the down wind thermal still holding from high to lower ground, they have good wind coverage back to their bedding area. This phase of our subject has been touched upon in a previous chapter, but it is of such importance it deserves some repetition by way of emphasis.

A prevailing wind, of course, cancels out all thermals. It also touches off deer reaction to these changed conditions. Forests do strange things to winds. A north wind may be channeled in a score of different directions, even though the set of the air currents is from the north. It may come spiraling around a ridge, moving east for some distance, south if the contour of the hills is favorable, west—just about any direction except north. This changes deer trailing habit.

Examine deer trails under these changed conditions and you see that these trailing habits have matched the wind change. A deer trail may be in use for weeks of stable weather conditions, with the morning and evening thermals regulating the traffic over it. But with this north wind blowing constantly, this trail may be abandoned. Others are selected because they give better wind coverage under the changed weather conditions. The one constant in all this is the deer's predilection to traveling nose-to-wind.

This prevailing wind may send him in a round about fashion, following that air current as it is affected by the contours of the hills. But follow it he will, swinging back and forth as he approaches the feeding area, moving along other routes as he returns to his security cover. Deer trails will outline these seemingly purposeless wanderings. But once they are understood, you'll see that there is purpose all along the line.

Prevailing winds, however, may change bedding areas. But the ritual of deer travel is a constant, always nose-to-wind.

A wind over deer territory is often a tricky proposition to assess for proper hunting. You may believe that you are hunting carefully into the wind, with no chance of it betraying your presence, but don't be too sure. Any time deer move out unaccountably, suspect that they have been tipped off by the wind.

A wind striking directly over tall trees may curl down and back, close to the ground, sending hunter scent over a wide area. Severe storm winds driving across deer territory have their own peculiarities with which you must be entirely familiar for it outlines peculiarities of deer behavior. When a storm wind strikes over a ridge or line of trees, an air cushion is created in front of such an elevation. The current is deflected up and over. Beyond the edge of the forest or top of the ridge, this deflected wind turns down, quite often double in velocity. It strikes the forest or lee of the ridge from one hundred to as much as three hundred yards beyond the original deflection. Here, contrary to the usual supposition, is the unprotected spot. But directly behind the ridge or line of trees, there *is* a sheltered area, affording greater protection from the storm for the simple reason that the deflected wind bypasses this section.

Here, in an area of crosscurrents, the backwash of the storm, so to speak, the deer bed. These storm sheltered beddings, even at the expense of reiteration, are not too far down slope, nor are they found in the deep, cold canyons.

There is an almost endless variety of shelter spots created by a storm. A ridge lying lengthwise to a storm wind is inhospitable to deer on both sides and top, regardless of feeding attractions or security cover. But at the lee end of such an upland, there is the inevitable shelter. This will be selected for bedding during a storm, a place to wait it out.

This waiting out a storm by deer is no mere figure of speech. When an old stinker of a cold, disrupting storm is growling across the deer cover, the game feeding habits may be entirely disrupted. Deer take shelter and wait.

When the weather clears *after* a storm, sending the thermal wind drift up slope, up the valley and draws, deer move out to feed. Quite often this may be during a mid-day period. For the thermal normally associated with feeding is night. More to the point, having sheltered during a storm which may have curtailed their feeding for one, two, or three days, they are hungry. This explains the little understood action of deer and other game feeding at all hours of the day immediately after a storm.

Deer habit falls into predictable patterns, once you understand the direct tie in with weather. All that remains, really, is to relate them to your own hunting—tie your hunting to the same pattern. It becomes obvious that under stable weather conditions, you must follow game on trails, in the direction they normally move at a specified time of day. You may hunt toward bedding grounds, starting in early morning, *before* the thermal reversal comes. You can still hunt the outward movement of deer until late evening or poor shooting light cancels out your efforts. But you cannot reverse this hunting routine with any expectation of more than casual success.

During mid-day under stable weather conditions, you must be on the high ridges, the uplands. For now, with the set of the thermal from low to high ground, it is the only area giving *you* a chance to use the thermal to advantage.

In rough weather, you should hunt the sheltered sections of range, the lee side of the ridges and forest facings. Clearing weather gives you your best chance, regardless of time of day, directly in the feeding areas.

You and I will take these segments of deer hunting and put them together chapter by chapter in this book. At times there will be repetition, but the separate parts must be tied together to make a workable whole. A good starting point is with "Deer Hot Spots," where the over-all seasonal picture of weather is tied in with feeding and shelter. This is our next consideration.

Chapter 12

Deer
Hot
Spots

ALL wild animals—the tiniest shrew to the largest buck—are concerned with just a few essentials: food, warmth, and sheltering concealment. Warmth, of course, is the primary requirement all along the line. It touches off a chain reaction from early spring until late winter. Warmth during the growing season is the spring magic which sends lush deer browse skyrocketing. It loads many of the hardwoods with nuts. Wild fruiting trees and vines are always on the receiving end of this. Sections of deer cover which have the most sunlight not only produce the most abundant harvest, they also produce the most nutritious food as well.

Always, when you check a section for deer activity, you'll find that the areas which are the more shaded over a large segment of range have the least game. No deer territory is uniformly populated with game. Some sections are comparatively barren of all wildlife, from squirrel and ruffed grouse to lordly bucks. Adjacent to these barren sections of cover there are favored localities densely populated with deer and other wildlife. These are the hot spots both literally and figuratively. For quite often these sections of cover receive 5 to 10 degrees more warmth than the less favored areas.

You may like wilderness hunting, well away from other hunters.

Perhaps it is still hunting where you cat foot along the hardwood ridges, a big buck in mind. You may be a trail watcher. You may get your greatest thrill out of organized deer drives. But regardless of what type deer hunting you prefer, you must be able to recognize these hot spots if you are to make them pay off.

The favored territories of deer are usually those areas having a southern exposure. This is country rising to the north, northwest, or northeast. This, as you see, covers a lot of deer hunting territory, but not all. There are sections, easily identified, where buffer ridges or heavy timber shut out the sun from the south, making for a cold, inhospitable region. But, you may ask, aren't all these slopes colder than the more sheltered swales, hollows and creeks? This would seem logical. Many fairly experienced woodsmen and hunters might string along with this proposition, even to the extent of camping in such seemingly sheltered areas. But those learned men, the meteorologists have put the finger on these woodland hot spots by the simple expedient of testing ground contours with a thermometer.

Sure, elevations show an average temperature drop of about 3.5 degrees for each thousand feet of increased height. This is the over-all average. Temperature measurement, however, doesn't show a uniform progression from high to low as one moves up slope. During cold weather there will be as much as 10 degrees difference in warmth on 300 to 400 feet of slope, measured from the foot, with the ground actually colder at the creek bottom. This is caused by air drainage. Cooling air, like water, flows downhill, slopes, valleys, and draws. Obstructions cause it to pool very much as water does.

This pooling in draws and swales is so distinct that often the frostline kill shows on an individual bush, brown to about half its height, vivid green above this. See how all this adds up? Over the season the favored areas have warmth, food, and shelter. There is no essential here which is attractive only to deer; this is the environment of *all* wildlife. I especially make this point because it is the identification mark of the hot spots. You cannot break these over-all requirements down into individual segments. They must be added up to a total over-all requirement if they are to serve your hunting.

Security cover alone will not afford any great amount of good deer hunting unless it is tied in with the other essentials which go to make up a hot spot. Experienced hunters all know of a certain seemingly attractive section of deer cover scarcely worth considering because the game avoids it. They remember sections hunted where the only sign of deer were a few tracks passing through the territory.

One such piece of cover comes easily to mind. I hunted it in the Umatillas of northeastern Oregon. Mule deer were on the move, migrating from their summer to winter ranges. Note, please, that this migration was from high mountain range to the lower elevations, sometimes a drop in elevation as much as 5,000 to 7,000 feet. Within this spread of elevations, however, there were sections where the lower areas received the most cold.

Favored spots were pinpointed along the travel route with beds, areas where the moving deer had paused to feed for two or three days before continuing their migration.

One section of forbidden territory was a long, steep, heavily wooded canyon trending to the east. The high wooded slopes shut out the sun. I remember this bit of forbidden woods intimately because it lay across the migrating route of those Mule Deer, and I took up the tracks of a very large deer on the high opening rimming the wooded section, followed it down slope and up the other side, emerging on the southern exposure of this mountain range.

During this passage I was struck with the coldness of the frozen woods, the lack of deer stopping in this inhospitable region. The tracks, of course, were an open book, telling me just how deer responded to the area. Cross it they did, by the hundreds, but their line of travel indicated a desire to put this section behind them as soon as possible. The snow had lain here for weeks. The canyon had a cold drag of a bone-chilling air current from the higher elevations.

Emerging on the south ridge and slope, the contrast proved startling. Tracks showed that the deer had slowed their travel, fanned out to browse on the bitterbrush, juniper, and bunchgrass. Those huge fresh tracks I concerned myself with turned off into a sun-warmed thicket of small sugar pine. I moved in on him cautiously, taking the better part of an hour to cover seventy-five yards. I found him, as expected, snugged down for the day *after* he had made a tight little trail loop to get air coverage from his backtrack. I managed to drop him in his bed, a beautiful four-point buck.

Here on the sun-warmed, south trending slope I put up several blue grouse. The squirrels were about their cone cutting. It all added up to this: one section of cover loaded with all types of wildlife, an adjacent section totally barren. Find suitable deer habitat and you find territory preferred by all game. Contrarily, when you are looking for good deer hunting, an abundance of rabbit, squirrel, ruffed grouse can tip you off to the hunting worth of an area.

I recall one such territory I discovered while hunting ruffed grouse. During the day's tramp I placed my hands in six large deer beds, all warm and smoking fresh. I jumped cottontails in the tangles of berry vines about the small ridge openings. I found an abundance of small birds at their leaf turning. When the deer season opened, I paid this section a return visit. By eight o'clock my partner had a beautiful six-point buck.

Later in the winter I returned here for a week of solitary hunting with camera and binoculars. It was still the same hot spot of the earlier season. Ruffed grouse in the cover complemented the rabbit population, the innumerable small birds. Big bucks were moving at all hours of the day, it being the rutting season.

While my primary concern was picture making, I spent time tracing out the boundaries of this game territory. Walking north for three hours, I found the entire section a deer hot spot. I turned west for two hours, then south for an equal length of time, outlining the boundaries of this favored territory. Subsequently I worked my way out of this territory, dropping down the north trending slope of a heavy reforesting. I became immediately aware of the change. Here I found little sign of any game. A few small cedar showed indications of *deer rubbings* where bucks had taken the *velvet* from their antlers in August. Deer droppings were old. The casual browsings were old, brown tipped, showing only mid-summer use.

Tramping the water courses where creeks angled out of the southern slopes, the favored territory, I found plenty of fur sign, but not in a uniform concentration. Beaver dams were in those sections of waterway which received the most sunlight, where no crisscross of tributary streams pooled the cold air moving down valley.

110

The boundaries of this hunting hot spot covered at least three miles of slopes and gently rolling hills. All this favored territory had sufficient elevations to give good air drainage. The north limit had a distinct line of demarcation, the lush growth ending on the north slope. To the west and east this wasn't so readily apparent. But there was a feathering out of the rich browse to both the east and west in the steeply wooded sections. This, primarily, because these sections like the north, received less all around seasonal sunshine.

All deer hunting hot spots are not as extensive as this one. But they all have the same factors of warmth, shelter, and food, regardless of size. Sometimes, you'll find them linked together across a deer range. Sometimes, small sections of inhospitable cover intervene. In any event, you'll find no section of cover uniformly populated with deer. It is almost impossible, as a matter of plain hunting fact, to find more than two or three extensive hot spots in any section affording a day's hunting. This, of course, is all the more reason why you should be able to recognize the type of cover affording you your best chance. Such hunting knowledge can save you a lot of profitless effort. It also underscores the desirability of getting repeat performances in those sections which have proven productive on former hunts.

Experienced woodsmen may point out a spot of cover and say, "That looks like a good place for a buck." Pin him down and he'll probably not be able to tell you the reason for his opinion. But don't bet he isn't right. For experience is behind that observation. In all probability he is pointing at a small segment of cover which has all the elements of a deer hot spot. Perhaps the section he indicates is only an acre or so in extent; it still has those basic requirements: warmth, shelter, and food, either immediately available or within reasonable distance.

Sometimes you'll find deer pocketed in hot spots covering very little territory, a half acre or so of sunny slope. Sometimes, of course, they may bed a half mile or so from the section producing the best browse or other food. But, being essentially lazy, they move no farther from the more open feeding areas than required for the two other segments of a hot spot, warmth and shelter.

Large, individual bucks tend to be solitary before and after the rut. So when you find exceptionally favorable cover, you have probably found deer territory worth your best hunting efforts.

111—Deer Hot Spots

I have one buck, a big three pointer, spending his winter with only two other deer, a doe and fawn, scarcely a half mile from where this is being written. The outline of this small hot spot is traced each time we have a cold frosty night, for here the frost is first to leave in the morning. And, while adjacent slopes are still rimmed with ice, the sun's magic has worked its charm on this south slope.

Walk through the forest and you'll find the ground frozen underfoot in the draws and hollows where the cold air pools. But, when you come to this small segment of south slope, you'll notice an increase in warmth at once. You'll also notice more bird activity, squirrels about their business of cone cutting, or if it is in late winter, you'll find them digging out their concealed cones and nuts.

If this buck with his small complement of does and fawns is driven out by stray dogs, as frequently happens, he will return within a few days. When a buck is killed here during the autumn hunting, it isn't long before another pre-empts this favored territory. It has been good hunting for the past twenty years to my personal knowledge. And, unless the cover is destroyed, it will be a prime place to find a buck twenty years hence. It's no happenstance that those trails about the warm slopes here are cut deep by years of use; it's that kind of cover.

Best starting point in developing ability to recognize these favored bits of deer territory is to watch the countryside as you drive along a highway after severe weather. Notice the forbidden stretches of territory covered with unmelted snow, old snow, iced over. Stop for a few moments, get a touch of the cold air. See any amount of bird life? Any rabbit or deer tracks?

Farther along, if you continue your drive, you'll come to the south exposure of gently rolling hills, or perhaps the lee of a heavy forest. At once you'll notice a greater warmth. There is more of a soft spring-like feel to the air. This is literally a hot spot, with good air drainage. You'll notice more birds about, more evidence of rabbits, more deer tracks.

Once you are able to recognize the basic differences between hospitable and inhospitable deer territory, you'll marvel at the simplicity of classifying the good sections of deer range. This hunting knowledge is the foundation upon which you'll base *all* your hunting, whether it is driving, still hunting, or trail watching.

Chapter 13

Deer

Habit

THE experienced hunter who has spent plenty of time studying his quarry has intimate knowledge of deer habit upon which to base his hunt. It's trite to say that the woods are an open book to such a hunter, but it is none the less true. He knows deer habit, forward and backward. When a full moon hangs low in the late autumn sky, touching the scarlets, browns, and gold of the woodlands with an overlay of silver, this experienced hunter is not only mindful of the beautiful setting for his hunt, he also knows the effect of that moon on plans.

Rain, shine, storm, all these have their effect on deer hunting, regardless of whether you plan to drive, still hunt or trail watch. Given a full moon over the deer cover, your quarry feeds during the entire night, then is securely bedded in the thickets before good morning shooting light.

Deer hunting plans based on the normal morning and evening feeding periods, under the circumstance, are futile. You must appraise chances in accordance with changed conditions. With the full moon in the autumn sky, they travel at night, feeding, playing, holding high revel on the ridges and in the open glades.

One autumn evening, belatedly caught out in heavy forest, I waited moonrise before continuing my walk to camp along an old logging road. This waiting turned up a very unusual deer hunting adventure. Coming to a small opening in the trees, much less than a half acre in extent, I saw movement in the moonlight. Waiting and watching, this movement resolved itself into three deer playing. They jumped over the small wild rose bushes in their path. Other deer joined them, bouncing back and forth.

The full moon, now well above the ridges, made this opening a bright place of shine and shadow, the deers' actions easily seen. Round and round they went in a sort of woodland tag. Occasionally they would pause, two of them would stand facing each other on their hind legs, clawing with their front feet, then they would bounce away and two others would go through the same routine.

I watched them frolicking for the better part of an hour before they finally quieted down and began to browse.

These deer, playing and feeding during the entire night, would be securely tucked away in some favored thicket come morning. Still hunting them under the circumstances would be profitless, unless you were directly on their bedding grounds. Trail watching wouldn't pay off either. Your best opportunity would be in driving the thickets, something fully covered in another chapter. Here, the point I wish to make is that you must tie in your hunting with deer habit to be successful.

Under stable weather conditions deer moving out to feed in the evening usually have the does and fawns in the lead, the bucks bringing up the rear. Sometimes, the buck will be much later than the lesser deer in coming to a feeding opening. In my orchard, where I constantly have deer under observation, I have clocked the interval between the first arrival of does and fawns and the arrival of the mature bucks as being as much as three-quarters of an hour. This underscores the necessity of being extremely cautious in your area or trail watching, once you have game before you. No matter if they are of no particular trophy worth, wait it out, unmoving. If you touch off the alarm now, that trophy buck you dream about will not give you a chance for a shot.

This trail movement, incidentally, with the does and fawns in the lead as they move out to feed, has a very practical reason for being. It's a pattern of deer behavior shaped by necessity.

You may wonder why mature bucks and does shouldn't be casually mixed on the trails. The reason for this is not, as I recently read in a learned magazine article, because the does and fawns are less cowardly than the bucks. Such reasoning only serves to confuse an inexperienced deer hunter. Bucks are extremely cautious, but no more so than does in heavily hunted territory. They are all equally courageous. I doubt if any deer can be called cowardly. When there is an occasion for a display of courage, deer have it in full measure.

All deer habit is forged of necessity and has been in the process of formation over the ages—long before they were even hunted with bow and arrow by primitive people. Their trailing habits were formed by their natural predators. Buck deer, better equipped for both fighting and flight, are the rear guard.

The rear of the herd is the most vulnerable part when they are moving out to feed. Traveling nose-to-wind, as they take advantage of the thermal, fair warning is had of any danger before them. But predators trailing the herd is something else again. They could, if the small, the weak, the does often heavy with fawn, were at the rear of the herd, easily pull down one. But between these and their hereditary danger the mature bucks are interposed.

A cougar lying in wait on an overhanging tree or rocks beside a deer trail makes a beautiful picture, but it is a picture and nothing more. With deers' predilection to travel nose-to-wind, that predator would be detected on its stand long before the intended victim came within range. Snow sign, where one of the big cats have pulled down deer, usually indicate a much different approach to the problem. Reading such sign, I have always found them approaching an individual deer, usually on the feeding grounds, keeping their quarry up wind. Usually, too, they take full advantage of the least cover—a bush, small tuft of grass, to come within springing distance. If a cougar can manage to come within thirty feet, it depends on speed to put it on its quarry before the deer can get under way.

The late "Cap" Wyant of Bandon, Oregon, once had a ringside seat when a cougar attempted to pull down a three-point buck. The process was much as I have described it, except in this instance the deer got under way before the big cat made contact. He gave up after missing the buck by inches, and stood for a moment watching the deer move out, a picture of feline frustration.

Buck guarding a deer herd moving out after feeding? Mr. and Mrs. George Welch saw a doe, two fawns, and a forked-horn buck feeding on an open hillside above their ranch house. A deeply cut wash angled down the hill full length of the opening. It was covered with an impassable barrier of blackberry vines, save for one spot used by the deer in their comings and goings.

After a casual mid-day feeding, it being a stormy day, the doe, one fawn, and the buck crossed the wash. Unalarmed, they browsed casually up wind toward the protection of a sheltering thicket. One fawn, however, must have gotten signals mixed. It continued to feed across the wash after the rest of the small herd disappeared. Discovering them gone, its head came up as it listened, trying, apparently, to locate its companions. At this juncture the buck reappeared in the small opening. The fawn trotted by him, jumped the wash, followed by the buck.

Don't come to any sentimental conclusions about this buck showing parental concern about one of a woodland family, for the facts support no such idea. This buck had an instinctive urge to protect the rear of the moving herd, nothing more. It wasn't in his scheme of things to have a lesser deer trailing him.

Usually, when deer are moving into a feeding area or are out after feeding, they have a thermal wind drift to give them exact news coverage of the territory ahead. Down wind, however, they have left a plain scent trail. This scent pattern, laid down as they come out to feed, is their greatest concern. It not only outlines the time of their travel, but the direction and probable time of return.

The danger here which conditions their travel has been established by their predators. With the deer moving back toward their bedding, even after a thermal reversal, there are small segments of the trail having poor wind coverage. Predators could move in on them at these points without being detected unless security measures are taken. Here, again, there is a herd setup which precludes any great amount of surprise raiding. Mature bucks noramlly leave the feeding area quite some time before the does, fawns, and lesser bucks take to the trail. These bucks have time to travel full length of the trail before the other deer move. The scent pattern of their going is followed unvaryingly by the other deer when they move out after morning feeding.

Danger, such as a predator, or hunter, may make those bucks

turn aside from the normally traveled woodland pathway. When this occurs, other deer follow them in their devious wanderings until they are guided to other, and apparently secure bedding grounds.

Trail watching mornings, you'll probably have sight of a buck *before* you see does and fawns, if your stand is selected with due regard to the wind drift. An evening session will usually afford you sight of does, fawn, spike bucks *before* seeing a larger one.

When deer are following a scent pattern laid down by another deer, they usually travel with head fairly low to the ground. It's a mistake to think this gait as a sneaking out, if by this one means concealment alone. Surely, a deer probably has some thought of concealment in mind, but the fact remains that he has his nose on a scent pattern as he moves so effortlessly through the woods with his head well down.

There is yet another consideration: When you see a deer moving in this manner, ten chances to one he has not only a scent pattern of another deer before him, but he has been alerted by a hunter whom he hasn't surely located. Carrying their head low, they are enabled to see better below the bough line of snow laden trees. Beyond this is the matter of noise and convenience in moving. Head up, a big buck with a noble rack of antlers makes plenty of noise in the brush, a dead giveaway to any experienced deer hunter.

Deer have one unique gait about which hunters often speculate, a slow, cautious walk with the game picking up its feet as if it were walking on eggs. This is not just a stylized manner of moving, with no practical aspect, for there is always something of practical value to the game itself in any observed action.

Time after time I have watched deer move out with this mincing gait, this stylized manner of walking. Then one autumn day, watching a buck cross a maple glade, I was struck with the lack of noise he made. The ground was littered with a treasure of golden maple leaves, yet, this buck moved cautiously across the glade, every sense alert, making but little noise.

I watched his feet with my binoculars. Each time he stepped his toes were pointed directly at the ground. Then as the foot was placed it was brought slightly forward. So precisely was the gentle lifting and shoving under those leaves, they were scarcely disturbed. In recovery the process was just the reverse, the foot coming high and free above the litter of leaves, all done very quietly. Later, examining the tracks, I found no leaves crushed.

This was an alerted deer. His first intimation of a hunter is either scent or unusual noise, something foreign to the woodland, such as the harsh breaking of a large limb, *travel off-trail* or in the worng direction for the time of day. When this sound is pinpointed, and while the deer is moving out, he wants to keep in contact as a matter of reassurance. He cannot do this if his own movements are very noisy, hence, the stylized walk which is very quiet, even in the noisiest cover.

When you see deer moving in this stylized walk, so beautiful in execution, rest assured you have been detected. Freeze into complete immobility. Quite often he will stop and listen, trying to locate the noise which alerted him, and with which he had lost contact, thus affording you a very easy standing shot.

Deer have several sounds they make in communicating with other deer. Probably the most familiar is the snorting or blowing. Some sportsmen will tell you that only bucks blow, with the does being mute. This is erroneous. Both the does and bucks blow when alarmed. This blowing is definitely a warning signal and will carry for several hundred yards. Woodsmen often imitate this snorting to bring a buck's head up for the shot when it is feeding in shoulder-high browse.

With very little practice, you can imitate this warning signal. The breath is expelled in an explosive manner, the call completed by a harsh blowing. I have stopped deer on trail time after time by using this warning call. One precaution you must remember in using this call, never overdo it. If properly done, one signal will usually stop a deer. More than this may touch off the quarry, speeding it up instead of slowing it down.

Another warning signal of deer, often used in connection with their blowing, is the drumming on the ground with a front foot. This is also used as a warning when something attracts a deer, but it is unsure of its nature. It is more apt to be used alone when the object of suspicion is not moving, such as a hunter on trail watch or stand. Quite often, under these circumstances, a ravel of hunter scent touches off the deer, or a bit of unrepeated movement. Then it sharply strikes the ground with its front foot, trying to drum up a bit of confirming movement, and at the same time warn other deer.

I have watched deer drum and blow when alarmed, moving back on the trail a short way, then going through the routine again. Quite often this is a doe separated from her fawns, and with hunter scent before her to warn of danger. During the entire routine of drumming and blowing, the tail is held very erect, quite often the hair stands up on the neck, a beautiful sight a hunter always remembers.

Deer shed their antlers during mid-winter, depending on locality. This is the end product of a routine which starts in spring when the bucks begin to grow new antler formations. The does are always bareheaded, except in unusual, non-typical cases when they occasionally sport a modest head of antlers.

During the spring and summer, antlers have a hairlike growth covering them. This is called "velvet" and a buck is "in the velvet" before the antlers harden and are rubbed during mid-summer. This rubbing is usually attended to on the soft bark of trees, such as willow, cedar, small firs, or pine.

The actual shedding of antlers in mid-winter is a subject of much argument, even among experienced woodsmen. Most authorities believe that bucks knock off their antlers on a convenient tree when they become loose and annoying. I have actually witnessed a buck removing his unwanted antlers in mid-winter. This buck, a forked-horn, was walking along a deer trail I had under observation—hunting with a camera. A storm cascaded buckets of water into the bare winter trees and I sheltered under a dry hemlock trying for some pictures, but mostly waiting for a break in the storm so I could return to camp.

This forked-horn moved along the rain-washed trail, his ivory-tipped antlers agleam with diamond sparkles of water. Suddenly he paused, reached up with a hind foot and knocked off an antler. Then he shook his head, reached up with his other hind foot and freed himself of the remaining one.

I recovered those antlers from the trail and examined them critically. One showed a very small blood spot at its base; the other showed nothing.

Shed antlers provide very interesting data on winter ranging habits of deer. The seeming lack of shed antlers, which most authorities attribute to the fact that they are eaten by rodents,

I feel has another reason. They are not found because the average hunter is not observant. I seldom spend a day in typical deer cover without finding several.

One other deer habit I must touch upon, even at the expense of repeating myself. This is the solitary habits of truly trophy bucks. Sure, bucks range with the herd, especially during the rut. But the truly out-sized ones, those with beautiful racks of antlers, are both lazy and tend to be solitary before and after the rut. They may use the same feeding area as other and lesser deer, but they tend to more night feeding and solitary bedding. If they are within the area of other bedding deer, they select the most inaccessible part.

A hunter who downs one of these big bucks is usually a woodsman who devotes full time to the task—both in season and out. For he must know both the bedding and feeding habits of the individual deer; and believe me, *all* deer localities have one or more such bucks about which local hunters talk.

The pre-season hunting should be done either with a camera or it should be simply devoted to exploring the comings and goings of your quarry. You can trail watch, moving in closer to the bedding area until you establish the place where this outsized buck is on the move *before* dark. You can pinpoint his bedding area and explore the possibilities of driving him by cooperative still hunting with a partner.

You must remember that this buck about whom those hunters talk has successfully matched wits with all the hunting talent for years. But he is a creature of habit. Once jumped, his manner of getting away will afford clues to probable future actions. When he gives you a sneak, follow him. See what he has in mind. This may be a clue to posting a hunting partner on those woodland pathways when you try for him again.

Hunting alone, follow him when jumped, track him and watch the cover ahead as you move slowly and cautiously. For as surely as autumn sunrise on a multi-colored maple, he'll stop and con his back trail for evidence of pursuit, affording you a shot. For this is his habit, and it underscores the prime necessity of always keeping your hunting compatible with the habits of the game you hunt. There are no halfway measures if you are to depend on anything but luck for your kill.

Chapter 14

Reading

Trail

Sign

REGARDLESS of the type deer hunting you do—driving, still hunting, trail watching—you must know what your quarry has been up to for the past twenty-four hours. This is pinpointing the hunt. Beyond these requirements you must know the worth of a deer territory by being able to tell if it has been favored by game for the past several months. Tying all this together into an understandable whole, you have a yardstick for measuring deer activity in a given territory.

Notice the amount of deer tracks you see when you enter territory harboring deer. These tracks, all coming and going without seeming purpose, spell out deer activity—past, present, and future of this section of cover. You start with tracks, and with a deer down before your rifle, which is another way of saying *all* successful deer hunting begins with sign reading.

Suppose you and I examine some deer tracks to see what they might tell us of game activity in a section we plan to hunt. We find four different sets of tracks on a not-too-well-used trail between dense woods and a comparatively open section. Look at these prints carefully. They have been made by undisturbed deer. The back feet print upon or slightly over those of the front feet at their normal cautious walk. A buck shows drag mark quite

Trails lead out to the feeding areas, such as this orchard covered with snow. These deer, coming in to feed, will use the same trail for their withdrawal unless there is a drastic wind change.

often, if he is a large deer, when there is snow upon the ground. On bare ground this may be indicated by disturbed leaves.

With these things in mind, we examine the trail carefully. Here, where the three sets of tracks show the deer have moved into the heavy cover after feeding, we find the largest, most rounded track moved over the trail first, with the lesser tracks imposed on this larger set. That, remember, indicates a buck. To check it further we examine tracks of the herd moving out to feed. Here we find this large set imposed on the lesser tracks.

We know now that this herd consists of a buck, a doe and two fawns. We are interested in that buck. Some guides and woodsmen profess to know whether a print is made by a buck or doe by the shape of the track alone. Some will even go further and tell you the number of points this buck is carrying. This nicety of woodcraft is supposed to be a direct result of a large amount of experience. I have grave doubts of all this. For, if this is true, my own perception has not developed properly—even with a lifetime spent in top drawer deer territory, an avid interest to spur on my study of deer—winter, summer, spring.

The more rounded track is supposed to be that of a buck, and to a certain extent this is true. But it is not an unfailing indication of the deer sex. While you can be fairly certain that a large, well rounded track is that of a buck, a mature doe without fawns could also make the same type print. Two things are required for a round-toed track, plenty of weight and fairly rocky ground to abrade the hoofs.

If you find a large track with well-rounded toes and solitary, that would be good indications of a buck. More, if those tracks showed the characteristic drag marks, then you could be reasonably certain. More evidence of a buck is indicated when the tracks show a wider trailing from a center line.

A doe is more free stepping, with less strut in her walk than a mature buck. She picks up her feet cleanly, walks more to a center line, and being smaller, less fat, due to nursing fawns, the hoofs show less abrasion, are more pointed. Beyond these considerations you cannot go with certainty in establishing the sex of a deer by its tracks.

Deer tracks made when the game is ascending a steep hill appear shorter, more rounded than tracks made by the same animal on level ground. Conversely, tracks made during downhill travel appear longer because more pressure is applied toward the rear of the hoofs. Slipping can also lengthen downhill tracks. Obviously, to get a proper perspective of a set of tracks under review, they must be seen on several types of ground.

Deer movement is not always defined by clear-cut tracks. Quite often the sign you'll see is nothing more than a few leaves disturbed, a slight impression where the game has stepped. Some sign remains visible on bare ground for a considerable length of time. Other traces of deer movement disappear quickly. The success of your hunts depends on small segments of sign which have no great significance to a careless observer. It is easy for me to recall a not unusual example of this.

The place we hunted had every thing except good security cover. It consisted of several thousand acres of overgrown logging slash, with the brush not quite tall enough to afford good day bedding. The deer moved in to feed in late evening when weather conditions were stable. They fed during the evening and night, then retired to the second growth to lay up for the day. We arrived in this area immediately after the morning feeding period, prepared for a day of cooperative still hunting in the second growth. Dew still shimmered like diamonds on the cover. But these diamonds of dew were lacking in those places where the deer had recently fed and moved.

A study of this not too obvious bit of woodland information led us to change drastically our hunting plans. Instead of moving in and out of the heavy cover to the west, as they had done before, we found the deer using the security cover to the south of the logging slash, a drastic change in their normal routine for this area.

We didn't know the *why* of this change at the time. Later, however, we found that two other hunters had taken deer the previous day in the west security cover, causing the remaining deer to change their daytime bedding from this disturbed area.

In the logging slash proper the thick mat of weeds and grass prevented detailed reading of tracks. But the retreat of the deer was outlined by the disturbed brush, the broken spider webs, and the absence of dew on the used trails. My partner took a big four-pointer on what would have been a barren day if we hadn't read the available sign properly.

Actually, we had little to go on in establishing the best territory for our day's hunt—dew knocked off the brush, a spider web broken on one trail, a spider web stretched across another. We had to assume that deer had moved here instead of other animals, for it was prime deer territory. We assumed, too, that at least one or two bucks would be with the herd, it being close to the rutting season. And that is the way it turned out. Experienced hunter or not, you could have just as easily made the same deductions from the evidence offered, for this is not so much a matter of several years hunting experience as it is of becoming a trained observer capable of seeing in detail.

The point I wish to make is that there is nothing upon which an experienced outdoorsman bases his hunt which isn't also before the inexperienced hunter. The difference is in observation and interpretation, which is another way of saying hunter attitude.

I once encountered a hunting problem similar to the foregoing while hunting alone. Crossing an overgrown upland pasture of a hill farm I saw where some animal had passed through the territory, the evidence outlined in the dew-wet grass. Of course I couldn't be sure the dew disturbance was caused by a deer, but that was a logical deduction. Following the distinctly outlined trail I came to a heavily wooded bit of hill cover—excellent security cover for deer.

The trail angled around a hill and crossed some damp ground. Here, for the first time I got a good impression of the track, a solitary deer, a large track, and smoking fresh. In addition the damp earth held several older track impressions the same size as the fresh ones, suggesting that the overgrown fields of this abandoned hill farm had been used regularly for several weeks.

I followed the tracks, often losing them, then finding them again, because I made the obvious deduction that this deer moved toward the high heavily brushed ridges to day bed. This particular deduction was suggested by the stable weather conditions, with its thermal wind shift night and morning. This thermal set of wind, now coming down slope, gave him good news coverage of the high ridges toward which the trail trended. Within an hour, however, there would be a change, with the wind drift reversing itself and moving up hill, with the current coming off his backtrail to the bedding grounds. I knew that unless I caught up with him during the next hour or so, I had to be directly on those high ridges to successfully continue my hunt.

I moved cautiously, always on trail, knowing that the slight noises I made duplicated those of an unalarmed deer. He had almost reached his hideout when I came upon him. He was browsing casually, nose-to-wind, which gave him coverage of the bedding ground toward which he made his way. To get the easy shot he presented, at a range of less than forty yards, as it proved, every element of hunting outlined in previous chapters of this *guide* were brought into play. I had to not only read trail sign correctly, but I had also to know deer habit and thermal winds.

This beautiful five-pointer was bedding solitary, as I found out when I continued the short distance from the kill to the top of the ridge. Several old beds were scattered about in the dense huckleberry brush and sheltering hemlock.

He wouldn't have been solitary during the rut, or slightly before, make sure of that. Even the tracks would have been different. He would have moved with less caution, at a faster pace, with the individual prints showing a wider, more distinct placement. Quite often the dew claws show distinctly when deer move at a faster pace than the casual, unalarmed walk they usually use. Ten chances to one, if the time had been near or during the rut, this big five-pointer wouldn't have stopped to feed along the trail. Indeed, there is every chance that he would have abandoned this section in search of does. But when I cought up with him he still used a set of habits normal to the season *before* the rut.

When deer tracks litter the woods, a condition you'll find very obvious when there is snow on the ground to register them, it is very easy to over-estimate the number of deer in the territory. This is especially true under stable weather conditions, snow or bare ground. A storm cancels out tracks, leaving the cover ready for fresh sign. But stable weather conditions preserve them. I could have easily confused the tracks of my buck made two or three days before with those I actually followed. The older tracks looked comparatively fresh in the moist shaded sections of the trail, but the fresh tracks I followed printed on enough of the older ones to cancel out any thought of the trail being laid down by more than one deer. And the direct comparison showed the difference in the age of the tracks.

Once I showed two inexperienced hunters a deer trail leading into my orchard. I asked them to estimate the number of deer using it. They gave both the trail and orchard careful study, looking at the welter of tracks about the fallen apples upon which the deer fed each night. Their estimate ranged between fifty and sixty deer. Around midnight we went forth with a flashlight and counted noses. Thirteen deer were feeding in the orchard— four does, eight fawns, and a three-point buck. Earlier in the evening I had been on the receiving end of some good-natured razzing when I suggested that perhaps a dozen deer were visiting the orchard.

My closer estimate stemmed from a more realistic study of the trail sign. Those two inexperienced hunters saw *all* those tracks as being of the same age. They should have considered only those leading *out* of the orchard after the night feeding period. No esoteric woodcraft was involved, just a logical consideration of the problem presented by the evidence.

Deer had come into the orchard. They had moved out by the same trail, leaving plenty of trail sign. I simply discounted all tracks coming into the orchard, made a careful appraisal of those made when they left. It's the type of detailed observation you must make as a matter of course to keep your hunt productive.

A skilled deer hunter doesn't see the cover as a broad over-all picture of gold-splashed autumn trees, or perhaps the same territory under a mantle of snow. For him, each segment of the area stands out alone, separate and distinct. He sees the detail. This enables him to recognize the most minute disturbance in the cover he hunts.

This accuracy of observation must be habitual. It eliminates confusion as to old or fresh deer sign. For example, each summer in late August, long before the hunting season opens, bucks rub the velvet-like covering from their antlers. Signs of this activity show on the bark of small trees. Seeing this, many hunters assume that those bucks are still in this territory during the autumn and winter hunting. This may well be. But should it prove the case, they are there because the territory still affords good food, shelter, and security. Indeed, in the case of mule deer, they may be fifty miles away from those rubbed bushes.

You naturally look for fresher sign. Quite often this may be confused with "rubbings." For you'll find hooked bushes where an autumn buck has worked off some of his pugnacity before the rut. Such sign is usually comparatively fresh during the hunting season. If you explore, you may connect this with other confirming sign, such as evidence of feeding, fresh tracks, fresh beddings, and well used trails.

At first you may have trouble judging the freshness of a set of deer tracks. Those made on two succeeding days are often hard to evaluate under stable weather conditions. Look closely for differences in appearance. Don't consider just one individual track to the exclusion of others. Study an average piece of trail, knowing that a single track or even a half dozen may be so sheltered that natural weathering hasn't taken place.

Fresh tracks on bare ground show a glaze along the outer rim. The rest of the print shows the impact of weight. The lightest fall of dew registers on these prints, with the center of the tracks showing minute specks of moisture on the packed dirt. The glaze about the rim will now show small cracks which radiate toward the center of the print. After only a few hours the glaze will change color and lose some of its polished appearance.

Tracks in wet ground, exposed to the sun, change appearance rapidly. The impression becomes less sharp as the dirt about the print dries.

During a storm, it is quite evident that a track which holds its shape and with mud in it, is freshly made, for a downpour of rain will wash out the appearance of fresh tracks within a half hour. A snowfall, of course, obscures the outline. All this, as you know, pinpoints the time such tracks were made to *before, during,* or *after* the storm.

Your ability to read sign on bare ground is the mark of the expert. It can be applied to reading snow sign. Deer tracks in snow age very rapidly. One hour of extreme weather conditions can change a print's appearance more than the change made by twenty-four hours of mild weather. The fresh track in snow has a distinct ridge about it and disturbed snow crystals lie on the unbroken surface about the track.

If the track is made before sunrise, the displaced snow crystals will freeze before the track itself freezes. But a weak winter sun can melt these snow crystals in two or three hours to the extent that they appear as small ice pellets. You must, obviously, tie in all your sign reading with the weather. Beyond that you must consider the season, time of day, expected deer activity, as well as the activity which produced the sign under observation.

If you see tracks leading away from a feeding area under stable weather conditions, you *know* they were probably made immediately after good morning-feeding light. Late evening you'll find them in a contrary direction.

The ability to read sign accurately is really a very simple art. Its mastery depends upon a sharpened sense of observation, the ability to put two and two together and come up with four for the answer. You are well down the trail toward becoming an expert woodsman deer hunter, once you recognize that there *is* a sign reading problem which is comparatively simple to solve.

Chapter 15

The Deer Hunter's Tattle Tales

PROBABLY the most important individual discovery you can make is that deer territory is never silent. It is loaded with highly vocal wildlife. Pause. Listen. Wait it out for fifteen minutes, forty-five, an hour, two hours. Listen not only for the sounds of the game you hunt, but more important, listen to the noise of the small furred and feathered creatures in your territory. You'll find your deer hunting territory a busy, noisy place, full of scolding tattle tales. This constant tale carrying can be turned to good account in your deer hunting. It not only enables you to see more deer, it can also be the means of giving you easy shots.

Once, I remember, a red squirrel cut himself in on my deer hunt with unexpected results. This squirrel, by all the rules of the game, should have been secure in his den tree, dreaming of hazelnuts, or whatever squirrels dream about. Instead, he was up and bright eyed. My partner and I were doing some cooperative still-hunting-driving. He waited on a complex of deer trails, while I still hunted in detail the crimsoned maples. The big buck I so confidently predicted I would put out across the ridge didn't show. All this despite the fact that I had his hideout pinpointed to less than an acre of hemlock and maple thickets. The setup was perfect for a late evening prowl of his hideout, too.

A north wind canceled out the usual thermal wind drift until fairly late evening during the day. Then it died down and there was a slight uphill thermal until very late evening, before the down-drift thermal started. Our hunt had been timed with this thermal wind drift in mind. The trails leading away from the hideout came to a focus on the ridge my partner watched. With the right wind to direct this buck's going, his hideout hunted slowly, cautiously, and in detail, this old mosshorn was sure to do a sneak along one of those trails.

This supposition was such a certainty I scarcely needed the reassurance of placing my hand in his warm recently-vacated bed. I waited there, now, expecting action on the ridge my partner posted. I kept telling myself that this buck was just slow in sneaking along the trails. Something had to happen there. Nothing did. Slow minute piled on slow minute until the suspense became a tangible thing felt from my tingling finger tips to my pounding heart.

A squirrel barked in a hemlock tree seventy-five feet to my right, sandpapering my already taut nerves. I turned cautiously in his direction. I could see him in a late sunlight splash on the tree scolding furiously, his tail accenting his loud disapproval with a twitch each time he barked. I eased up my binoculars for a more detailed look about the base of the tree, where the deep shadow pools lay contrastingly dark.

Movement! A shadow detached itself from a darker shadow. It was our buck as big as life! Detected by the squirrel, he exploded into action, crashing out through the underbrush. I managed to tag him as he crossed a small fern opening scarcely fifty feet from where I stood.

If it hadn't been for a woodland tattle tale in the person of that red squirrel, I am quite sure this big buck would have given us the slip.

Deer, themselves, are not along the butt of this scolding and tale bearing. Quite often a hunter is on the receiving end of this woodland invective. When a tattle tale discovers you on stand, trail watching or still hunting, there is only one thing to do. Remain perfectly quiet. Eventually your tormenter will lose interest. If it is a deer which has discovered you, as frequently happens if you are sitting perfectly still, and you do not want the shot, remain quiet and watch carefully. Such situations can often be turned to your hunting advantage.

131—The Deer Hunter's Tattle Tales

One October day, while trail watching, a doe discovered me. She spent a quarter of an hour telling every wild creature within hearing that an intruder was in the woods. She blew. She stamped her front feet, trying to drum up a little movement to confirm her conviction that here was an unwanted visitor. But I remained perfectly quiet.

Once I noted that she flicked her large ears downwind below the trails. This spelled out the fact that she wasn't alone. In hunting I like this kind of tattle telling. I turned my eyes without moving my head, watching and waiting. A small cedar swayed below the trail, not as if touched with a casual draft of wind, but with more purpose. One minute, two, five. The doe continued to blow and stamp her feet. Below trail, well beyond her efforts, an occasional fern frond moved, telling me of both stealth and progress. Eventually I saw a sensitive black nose at the edge of the huckleberry brush. It quested the wind for signs of danger. Another cautious step and I turned and fired. The doe vanished as my shot echoed through the autumn woods.

This buck was surely a victim of woodland tattle telling. I doubt if I would have detected the slight swaying of that small cedar which alerted me to his coming. I doubt, as a matter of fact, that he would have come out if he hadn't been prompted by the antics of the doe.

All wild creatures give the alarm call in a universal language. When a deer snorts or blows, it has meaning not only for other deer, but for any wildlife within hearing. The woods are alerted, and it is a time to do strictly nothing, save watch and wait. For much more often than is commonly supposed, the success of a hunt hinges on a few bird notes, the blowing of a deer, the barking of a squirrel, the cluck of a ruffed grouse.

Once I had this exemplified in singular fashion. Still hunting alone, in an area where the horned and broken bushes indicated good buck deer territory, I saw no deer during the morning. Twice, however, I had heard the soft chuck of hoofs in the moist forest litter, even though I got no glimpse of game when I put out these two deer.

At noon, seated on a large fir windfall eating my lunch, I watched a maze of deer trails and reflected on my lack of hunting success. The breaks had been against me. One of those deer jumped during the morning left its bed less than twenty feet from me.

132

But the intervening huckleberry brush prevented me getting even a sight of it, much less a shot. The other ran along a small ridge, just far enough downslope to be out of my sight.

Sitting on the silver weathered windfall eating my sandwich, my attention was attracted by the antics of three Canada Jays making their alarm calls in some mountain willows. They hopped from branch to branch, peered down through the naked limbs at something below.

I eased my rifle into better position and waited. The camp robbers moved directly toward me, flying from tree to tree, scolding at something in the dense cover below them. Then out into a small opening, like the picture of a storybook deer, a big five pointer stepped. His head was well down as he unquestionably followed a ravel of doe scent along the deer trail. His antlers were dappled with autumn sunlight—an altogether regal sight. I got my chance at less than sixty feet, dropping him with a neck shot.

On another occasion a ruffed grouse alerted me to an unexpected hunting adventure, even though I didn't bag a buck. I was still hunting across a maple glade, half bemused by the riot of crimsons, browns, and scarlet blobs of color splashed on the maples this Indian summer day. Then the *pert! pert! pert!* of a ruffed grouse came from a jumble of hardhack and hazel—a typical mixed forest, such as you find in the best deer territory. I was convinced my slow, careful still hunting hadn't touched off the alarm, so I watched the cover ahead and awaited developments.

The grouse thundered out of the thicket, curved over the fern to drop in the brush behind me. Then the sound of movement came from two points in the brush the grouse had vacated. Suddenly there was a rhythmical clicking in the cover as purposeful as two fencers at foils. The brush agitated to the crashing and snapping of limbs. I knew the answer to this at once. So I skirted the draw to gain higher ground where I could better see the action.

Two great stags were fighting in the brilliantly-colored autumn forest. They slashed and parried viciously with their antlers, totally oblivious to their surroundings. Sure, I was tempted. Either of these fighting bucks would have made a trophy to gladden the heart of any deer hunter. But somehow I couldn't shoot, even though a woodland tattle tale had tipped me off to a pair of the most beautiful bucks I had seen in several seasons.

The list of woodland tattle tales could be extended much beyond those outlined here. They'll get your attention in season. Listen to their gossip. Watch their antics. Sometimes the seemingly unrelated activities of the small furred and feathered creatures and the game you hunt are very closely tied together. If a bird is alarmed, what alarmed it? If a squirrel scolds, what is the objective of his invective? Those questions should underscore your direct concern while hunting deer. For many times there is a direct payoff.

You can, of course, profitably cut in on the propensity of woodland creatures to heed and investigate an alarm by using a deer call. Under certain favorable conditions you can call a deer to your gun. It is best used in not too heavily hunted territory.

These deer calls, several of which are presently available, imitate the distress call of a fawn. In calling, mute the notes, repeat not more than two or three times. After an interval of fifteen minutes or so, call again.

My first use of a deer call brought a jay, a squirrel, and three chickadees to investigate. But, let it be recorded, two does also responded. Subsequently, I discovered that more does came to the call than bucks unless it is during the rutting season, when the bucks are with does and follow them as a matter of course.

A too persistent use of a deer call can alarm game to the extent that they move off. Remember that. In selecting a position for this type of woodland broadcasting, be sure you can command all the approaches to the area where you are doing your calling. In using a deer call, which is a play on the propensity of all wildlife to respond to the alarm of a woodland dweller, I think you'll be surprised how well it works in calling up *all* furred and feathered creatures. Calling is not a major way of taking deer, but it does work on many an occasion, especially when it gets the cooperation of the woodland tattle tales.

Chapter 16

Proper Noise
Helps Your
Deer Hunting

ALL deer hunters of any extended experience know that there are times under certain weather conditions when *all* game is hard to approach. There are other times, also, when the contrary is true. Few experienced hunters haven't been within very short distances of deer before putting them up. Such days are those when they flush ruffed grouse close-in and see squirrel and other small game at very short range.

These hunting phenomena are directly tied in with weather. To understand *how* weather affects your deer hunting, you must know *how* the game reacts to noise, something touched upon in previous chapters. More, you must disabuse your mind about the virtues of silence in deer hunting. There is a lot of fanciful tale telling done by exponents of the "Silent Indian" school of deer hunting. The noble Redskin, according to report, went about his lethal business of hunting without a sound. Many hunters have had this old classic drilled into them since they were large enough to take a gander at the family gun rack. When they were old enough to hunt, they *knew* all old timers and Indians had this uncanny woods ability which they dispaired of equaling. Only it just isn't so!

There hasn't been a hunter, old-timer or Indian, from Uncle Cro-Magnon down to the veriest tyro with a shiny new deer rifle who ever moved in typical deer cover without making noise. Deer, themselves, do not confirm to this noiseless classic of the hunting book, either. The closest any animal comes to being noiseless in its movements is the cougar, the bobcat, and to some extent the timber wolf—all traditional predators of deer. *So the most alarming situation for all deer is movement without a complementing sound pattern to identify it.* Like proof of this statement?

A friend of mine, an avid deer hunter, had several deer in a brushy enclosure which very closely approximated natural conditions. He spent a lot of time stalking those deer just to see how they reacted to noise. He wanted to know *why* on some days he often walked in close on them, while at other times they flushed wild, even though he was exceptionally quiet in his approach.

A doe gave him his answer. Quite often she would take her two fawns and slip away to a jumble of vine maple and hazel thickets. Here she would snooze away the day between feeding periods. Hiding away in this jumble of heavy cover, she provided the perfect test of his stalking ability. Time after time he would cat-foot along, parting the brush in front of him, easing it into the trail behind him, moving with much less noise than the deer themselves. Always, however, when he came upon this doe and fawns he found her with those huge ears funneled forward, black nose testing wind. She simply had no use for this ultra quiet stalking. Her attitude told him plain as plain could be that he should get some recognizable noise in his hunting.

When he moved slowly, making a reasonable amount of trail noise, duplicating the pace of unalarmed deer, his approach was much more successful. The swish of his soft hunting clothes on the bushes duplicated that of a deer's soft body pressed against the cover. The occasional snap of a twig was a familiar sound to the bedded doe. Under the circumstances my friend would come upon her at rest, those large ears drooped, as nearly sound asleep as a deer ever becomes.

When this hunting friend walked in on this bedded doe, making the loud crashes of an average hunter, moving at a fast pace, he always found her fully alerted, just as I noticed the response of deer in actual hunting. All this, it seems to me, indicates a very narrow range of noise in which a deer hunter can move with any hope of hunting success.

Noise above this narrow range touched off the alert. Below this

136

you are also subject to suspicion. And, if you achieved that hunting classic of movement without sound to identify it, it would be the most alarming to all deer under most weather conditions.

That narrow range of unalarming noise is not easily duplicated by the average hunter, unless he knows the why and how of it. For it takes plenty of soft stepping knowhow, plenty of thoughtful practice to make it become second nature. A hunter is often so close to the alarming borderline of sound which tips off his quarry, just a little adverse weather can cancel out his best efforts. There will be times, also, when the weather is working for him.

A good example of weather and concomitant sound patterns is an autumn Indian Summer day, after the first frost has touched off a four alarm blaze of color along the hardwood ridges. Forest litter is now soft underfoot; noise is subdued. Even the very mechanics of walking tend to fall into sound patterns deer recognize as their own and normal to the woodland.

This is the time when experienced hunters walk in on their dream bucks. But, always, there is a qualifying thought. Suppose a good lusty autumn wind stripped most of those brilliant scarlet leaves from the hardwoods. Then a hunter could see his deer at double the range and get a better chance for a telling shot. Yet, in the clutch, those naked trees would offer little if any advantage. Sure, you could see farther, and you would need this advantage under the circumstances. For those fully leaved trees which reduce visibility to a scant forty yards also subdue noise, muffle it, bring it within the narrow pattern of unalarming noise.

Leaves gone, a mixed forest, with a complementing mixture of evergreens, such as hemlock, spruce, pine, and fir are always a good hunting bet under adverse weather conditions. For such forests still retain their ability to soften approach noise of moving hunters.

A soft tracking snow is traditionally a good time for deer hunting, but not alone because it is soft underfoot. Few hunters, assessing the merits of a soft unfrozen snowfall realize that the snow clinging to trees overhead is perhaps more important to the success of their hunt than that which is under foot.

Sure, a good tracking snow enables you to read deer sign. It outlines the normal deer trails discussed in previous chapters of this *guide*. But, that which clings to the trees serves as a wonderful sound baffle when each branch is weighed with its ermine covering.

Your hunt is sewed up tight if you play it canny, for the weather is making it possible for you to easily travel within the narrow range of sound acceptable to your quarry.

Suppose you are hunting in average rolling hill country, heavily forested. Trees are covered with a recent fall of snow. There is no wind. Two related factors of hunter noise must be considered here. Under the circumstances, normal noise tends to soar. If you are below deer *after* early morning, they not only tend to get your hunter scent, but louder trail noise as well. The sounds will be louder to the game above you, perhaps emphasized enough to be well above the normal woodland range of noise within which you must operate in order to not alarm your game. Ten chances to one, if you work in close to deer on such a day, you jumped it while moving along a ridge or hill at the *same* elevation as your game, or you were higher than your quarry on the hill.

Frozen snow and a naked forest present the hardest combination a deer hunter has to contend with from the standpoint of noise. Sound glances off a frozen surface without losing any of its energy. Ponds, rivers, and lakes in your hunting territory have this same characteristic of sound deflection.

A gusty wind scatters hunter noise, sending it upward along the ridges one moment, completely canceling it out the next. If deer are bedded when these erratic winds begin to blow, they are likely to stand up, move back and forth as they keep nose-to-wind, test the air currents, listen, totally alert. They make hunting under the circumstances a very tricky, fascinating proposition. Best hunting technique when these erratic winds are blowing is to pace them—moving when the wind moves, remaining quiet when it dies down. Better yet, drive your favorable deer territory with some members of your hunting party posted on the escape trails.

When a gentle rain is falling, you have an excellent chance of taking deer. Rains not only soften the forest litter underfoot, it also is one of the best sound baffles a woodsman can have, injecting a beautiful pattern of noise itself into your hunting setup. This prevents your game from having full attention focused on the sound pattern you are making while moving through the heavy cover.

On several occasions I have been within four feet of wild deer in heavy cover. I was not only on trail when this happened, but I usually had a gentle assist from a soft falling rain. The sound of rain tap dancing on the huckleberry brush, dripping from the trees with an underlay of sound—a whisper, if you will—enabled me to move in close. Once, while hunting with Elzie Randolph, I took a three-point buck at fifteen feet in a huckleberry thicket. Once I actually touched a yearling doe and there was a witness to confirm the act.

I even hesitate to report this particular deer hunting circumstance because so many hunters reading this will feel it totally impossible. But, I have my witness. More to the point, I had the experience. I am also encouraged to tell of the experience by the many reports I have had from hunters using the techniques touched upon in this *guide*. They have *all* come within a few very short feet of bedded deer before putting out their game.

The particular morning I have in mind was right for the co-operative still hunting my partner and I were doing. A soft rain fell on the cover we hunted. He worked along a complexity of deer trails following a long ridge. I paced him on the secondary trail about seventy-five yards downslope. I eased around a clump of huckleberry brush, placed my hand on the rump of this yearling doe. She was standing facing upslope, watching and listening.

At my touch she exploded into action, snorting at every jump as she took off for the top of the ridge. Three other deer, a doe and two fawns, came out of the huckleberry brush about ten feet from where I stood. I think these extra deer accounted, in part, for me getting in close. The yearling doe expected noise in the immediate cover. The rain, of course, put my noise well within the narrow band of acceptable sound pattern. The rest of the episode followed as a matter of course.

Falling snow has much the same characteristic as rain in serving as a sound baffle. When a snow is falling over your deer hunting range, get out and hunt. You'll be surprised at the many times deer are jumped close in, sometimes in only a few short feet of you in heavy cover.

There are times, under certain weather conditions, when all noise is intensified. I am thinking especially now of those periods of thermal reversals, evenings and mornings, during clear stable weather conditions.

139—Proper Noise Helps Your Deer Hunting

No air current channels the normal noise of a forest during these reversals. No wind eddies or cross currents deflect or smother them. At these times a maple leaf ticking down through the trees is startling in its loudness. A breaking limb is an explosion. Such times are occasions when you must be extremely cautious, regardless of your over-all hunting plans for the day. Watch. Listen. Plan on being in favorable deer territory *before* the morning thermal slack occurs. Let the hunt come to you.

This morning thermal slack will last about a half hour. It usually occurs about the time deer have finished their inflow toward their bedding grounds. They'll not lie down for their day bedding until the reversal is complete, and the thermal drag of wind is from their backtrail.

These thermals as you know (see chapter 11, Wind Over Deer Cover) send wind drift downhill and valley, away from the higher ground from late evening until fairly early morning. Then there is a reversal which sends wind drift upslope all during the day. There is never a time during your entire deer hunts when you can ignore these basic facts, either from the standpoint of noise or hunter scent, if your efforts are to be at all successful.

The evening thermal reversal usually occurs very late in the day—about a half hour or so before the last of good shooting light, under stable weather conditions. This is a prime time for area watching, remaining totally still. The sound of deer feeding or moving is greatly intensified during the thermal reversal in the evening. Quite often this will give you an opportunity to pinpoint your quarry right up to the time of the shot.

It all adds up to this: you do not have extra opportunities to spare in deer hunting. The basic factors of success which are touched upon in this *guide* must be employed as a matter of course, if you want to substitute knowhow for luck in your hunting. For you must know beyond the least shadow of doubt *all* the factors working for and against you, or contrarily, for or against your canny quarry. To understand this particular basic deer hunting premise, there is no better starting point than in remembering that proper noise helps your hunt, especially when it is tied in with the weather.

Chapter 17

Still

Hunting

Deer

STILL hunting is considered a type of deer hunting where the cards are stacked against the sportsman who matches his woodcraft against the canny ability of a wise old buck. It makes full demands on all your hunting skills; be sure of that. Yet, when all this is said, there remains the very pertinent fact, often disregarded, that it is a very effective way of taking deer, even in heavily hunted territory.

Before getting into the intricacies of still hunting, however, let's establish a definition of terms. Still hunting, contrary to some reporting on the subject, is not so-called because the hunter remains in one spot—still. This confusion of still hunting ritual with trail and area watching is altogether too common. Still hunting is akin to stalking, save that the quarry is not spotted before the hunt begins. In still hunting you lay it on the line, careful step after careful step, with the object of moving in, jumping the quarry and getting the shot yourself, or perhaps setting up the shot for a cooperating still hunting partner.

All this, as you know, brings us directly back to the importance of knowing deer habit—game reaction to noise, pace, timing. Even at the expense of reiteration, you can never be entirely noiseless in the woods; you can never approach within shooting range of any deer *without* that deer being aware of your presence long before you are able to see it in heavy cover. The deception which you must use to get in close is the type discussed in previous chapters of this *guide—noise in place in reference to the time of day, pace, and place.*

Yesterday, I came in from a day of still hunting, that is, by the time I got my trophy out to my pickup, and home, it was definitely a full day. I want to tell you something of the problem for it is often typical of those confronting a still hunter. The woods were dry and noisy under foot. The section I selected for my hunting had many trees down from a storm of gale proportions. Yet, it was the haunt of some outsized bucks in which I became interested because they presented some very intriguing problems in hunting and woodcraft.

This territory is fairly heavily hunted with most of the outdoorsmen depending on orthodox driving for their deer. This driving is, in a measure, successful though it turns up a lot more does, fawns and immature bucks than top-drawer trophies.

I started my still hunting early in the morning, dropping into territory which had been driven less than a half hour *before* I began hunting. Two factors convinced me that the undertaking had a good chance of success, despite the noisy drive only recently in this cover. First, the drive produced no shooting at any of the stands in spite of all the fresh sign. Second, noisy drives, with all the shouting, pinpoint hunters, enabling a canny old buck to avoid them while remaining in the territory.

How do you start and where to still hunt under such circumstances? First, I studied the obvious feeding areas—several long ridges covered with black huckleberry, blackberry vines, and hazel. Beyond these low ridges a dense covering of red alder, hardhack, and hemlock threw a green mantle over a southern exposure slightly higher than the feeding area. I knew that two drivers had gone through this section, moving toward a stand posted on a fire scald slightly upridge from the heavy cover.

I started my hunting on a deer trail leading out of the feeding area. This, of course, conformed to a basic pattern—out toward the security cover in early morning. More, it conformed to another pattern directly underscored by the drive—there is no movement on trails between security cover beyond the time when they are normally used by deer after the morning feeding period.

Essentially, I was helped by those hunters making the drive, much more than hindered, for they had filled the woodland with noise easily identified by the game as that of hunters. They had so emphasized this that any slow still hunter, following a deer trail meticulously toward the security cover and beyond, was one up on those thoroughly alerted deer.

The first fifty yards of trail out of the huckleberry brush was a maze of down timber, alders growing up through it and vines crisscrossed. The deer trail I followed forced me to crawl at times, inching along, placing my rifle before me, always making some noise, to be sure. After about seventy-five yards of this and *an hour later,* I came to slightly more open woods. Please note the time element, for it is the heart of the hunt. I use the words slightly more open woods advisedly, for none of this section afforded more than twenty yards of view in any direction. Yet, after another hour and fifty more yards of trail, I put a five-point buck out of some low-growing hemlock. It was an easy shot, so much so, the kill came as an anti-climax to the still hunting.

After field dressing my trophy, I dragged him out to the logging road where the drive started. Then, while loading him in the back of my Scout four-wheel drive, the hunting party which had driven the section came through. They had completed two drives without taking a deer. They exclaimed over my good fortune, but went away shaking their heads when I explained *how* I had taken him by still hunting some of the territory they had recently driven.

This *how* of still hunting, very much like that of proper trail watching, is a very hard proposition to put across to deer hunters. It is especially hard for the deer hunter of limited experience to believe there is an effective method of moving in close to a deer in heavy cover, especially when the woods are tinder dry.

The biggest deterrent to effective still hunting is the inability of the average hunter to realize that there *is* a game pattern movement which he must duplicate in every particular to be at all successful. Watch an inexperienced deer hunter when he gets into cover which is really tough going, such as I hunted this morning. Here, where it is imperative to take each step with care, he fights the cover, thinking that once he has gotten into more open territory where the cover is easier to negotiate, he'll settle down to his still hunting. In the meantime, he has alerted all deer within the immediate vicinity. Now, regardless of his ability to still hunt beyond the tangle of cover which gave him trouble, there is no chance of him coming up with his quarry.

In still hunting, you must always remember that the most concealing cover, the hardest bit of territory for you to travel, is usually the hideout of deer, for the simple reason that it affords the best concealment and protection. Sure, you'll make more noise hunting such sections, much more than if you were catfooting along an open ridge. There are compensations, however. Deer also make more noise in this heavy cover. They are conditioned to hearing louder noise here than in the more open sections of the cover. This noise, regardless of its loudness, must conform to pattern—pace, time of day, wind direction. Get these right and your still hunting falls in place, regardless of the cover.

You know that there *is* a daily ebb and flow of deer along the trails. You must shape up your hunt to this. In the very nature of things, you are bucking the impossible if you go contrary to the flow of this traffic. But once your still hunting is *right* with the expected deer traffic, you are in for some surprises. The game will seem much less shy, at times even stupid, even slow to realize that you are not one of the herd and are actually a hunter.

During the rutting season there is more or less trail activity all during the day. Trail movement at this time may be in any direction. But usually it is confined to the main travel routes between sections of security cover. Usually, too, it is the largest buck which is on the prowl. In this connection I recall one day, while hunting with camera and binoculars, I counted thirty-five large bucks during the day's picture making.

Hunting under such conditions gives one extra still hunting opportunities. This, of course, doesn't indicate less cautious movement. Those slowly paced steps must become second nature before you are a competent still hunter. Obviously, this slow still hunting makes a direct contribution to your efforts. Indeed, you can measure the worth of your still hunting by the degree of tiredness experienced at the end of the day. If you finish the day comparatively fresh, you are in the groove. If you come into camp at the end of the day totally beat out, you are hunting too fast to be effective, trying to cover too much ground.

144

In duplicating the pace of your quarry in still hunting, remember that it is seldom a constant unvaried gait. A deer pauses often to scan his backtrail. He pauses to listen to some unusual sound. He has all the other deer within hearing pinpointed by the slight noise of their movements. Your pauses, which duplicate theirs, will be made for another purpose, yet they are very essential.

In still hunting, as you move cautiously along the trails, you'll open new vistas of cover, vistas which you must inspect and examine in detail, making sure before you move onward again that no deer is in sight. This is basic. For the object of your slow careful movement is to uncover new territory which may harbor deer. Until *all* possibilities of an exposure are exhausted, there is no good reason for you to move forward again.

This recommended slow movement of still hunting naturally brings up a question, how far should you travel in a day of still hunting, covering the territory properly, conforming to game pattern? I would put this distance as being not more than a mile or a mile and one-half. In difficult cover it will be much less. Such distances enable you to return to camp with a sharp edge on all your facilities. It gives you time to *see* all the territory in detail. When you move much faster than this still hunting, your attention is more devoted to hiking than to hunting. There is a phrase credited to an Indian which summarizes this slow pacing of your hunt excellently: "walk a little, look a lot."

Still hunting with a partner underscores all the points previously touched upon and recommended for the solitary hunter. In addition, there are other factors which must be considered. Where two hunters are working a piece of cover, cooperative still hunting, they must not only pace the game they hunt, but also keep their own positions positively oriented at all times.

In cooperative still hunting one hunter may move along the top of a heavily wooded ridge, following the usual deer trails, and have no doubt there will be deer tracks here, in good game territory. Often these trails are just faint markings in the forest litter. Quite often they are very distinct pathways. He follows in the general direction of those trails, while a partner paces him at the bottom of the slope, perhaps fifty yards apart. Deer jumped by either hunter is often put across to the other.

When either hunter comes to cross trails, pathways which cut into the general trail pattern from the direction of the other still hunter, he should remain there, absolutely quiet, until he is sure that his partner has passed beyond this secondary cross trail.

This cooperative still hunting is probably the most effective of any method for taking deer in average heavy cover. But there must be cooperation indeed. For example, when two still hunters are working a bit of territory, they are constantly evaluating deer sign, fresh and old. Quite often the tracks of a worthwhile deer cut through the area of one of the hunters. These tracks are smoking fresh on a secondary deer trail leading directly toward the area where the hunter's partner is pacing him. If at all possible the hunter with the fresh sign before him, should move into position to put hunter scent along the trail of this deer. More, he should turn aside, momentarily, from his primary direction, and work this trail a short distance toward his partner. And, if his partner is meticulous about waiting it out for a short time when he comes to a cross trail, he'll probably get action.

On several occasions, hunting with a knowledgeable woodsman, I have worked this scheme, or been on the receiving end of the buildup when my partner put up the deer on those cross trails— either by careful still hunting toward my section for a short way, or given the quarry the scent of hunter to ponder.

The controlled use of hunter scent to flush game is much less appreciated than it should be as an aid for putting out reluctant deer in heavy cover. But quite often this is the best way of moving deer from the security cover where they are waiting out the hunt, fully alerted to your presence.

On one occasion, hunting with a partner, I managed to put the 'fixings' on a big four pointer by the simple expedient of staying below a half acre of dense hazel and small hemlock while my hunting partner moved in above this heavy cover. Here he stopped and waited, with the wind directly from him into the heavy cover. From the wind direction, down slope, I assumed that the deer would bed about midway up slope in the thicket. Fresh tracks leading into the section showed just one solitary deer, probably a good-sized buck.

So there we were, one covering the thickets from above, the other below, cooperative still hunting at its best. In position, we waited. I could see my partner's red hat through the multi-colored autumn trees. He, by the same token, could see me below the heavy cover, standing where I could watch not only the lower edge of the cover, but the farther outline of the thicket as well.

I expected the deer to move out along this farther edge for the simple reason that this trail would give him good wind coverage, assuming that we did have game before our rifles. We waited ten minutes, then a half hour, for such setup cannot be rushed. I was almost on the verge of moving on when I heard a twig snap, just this one bit of noise and nothing more. It seemed indicative. A deer could have stood up the better to evaluate the constant hunter scent coming into its hideout from upslope.

Nothing happened. Nothing for another ten minutes. Then I saw a bush shake slightly, contrary to the wind direction. Another bush farther along the hillside showed a slight agitation. It was our quarry moving out as expected, nose to the wind, on the far side of the thicket. A big four pointer stepped out of the concealing cover. I caught him just back of the shoulder with a heavy .348 Winchester, 200 grain bullet. He was a beautiful trophy.

In this type of cooperative still hunting, it is best, if at all possible, for only one hunter to be moving at once, with the other watching cover ahead of his partner's position. Quite often, if two hunters have agreed upon this procedure *before* the hunt, as they should, each will see opportunities for watching or stalking which can best be exploited by his partner. For example, while still hunting with a partner in Oregon's fabulous Umitillas, we found the tracks of three deer moving into a very dense pine thicket. I was directly on the tracks. My partner paced me about fifty yards to one side. I paused at the edge of the thicket until I knew he was far enough ahead to cover the exit trail; then I moved in, jumping a doe and two fawns.

If you deduct from all this that good, cooperative, still hunting deer partners are jewels without price, you are very right. Cherish such a partner. Hunt with him. Eventually, he and you will exploit a given still hunting situation as a matter of course. Anything requiring close cooperation will find both you and your still hunting partner knowing just about what the other will do without signals, even without thinking about it very much.

You'll not speculate about whether it is your turn to work a heavy piece of cover while your partner moves cautiously around it to cover the exit trail. No, you'll see the logic of either your moving

Author dragging a buck out to his Jeep. The deer had been field dressed. The distance to the Jeep, less than fifty yards. It is not recommended that deer be dragged for any great distance on bare ground.

in or your partner. If you *do* move in, you'll not have to wonder whether he is in proper position. He'll be there because it is the place for him to be. For both of you subconsciously have evaluated the wind, the game trails, everything which suggests the *best way* of handling this particular bit of cover.

In this cooperative still hunting you cannot be selfish, wanting the honor of the shot. The hunt must shape up logically. Once this is realized, the rest is comparatively simple for the actual stalking is indicated by the exigencies of the hunt itself. You keep within the pattern of acceptable noise. You keep within the pattern of game movement as to time and pace. This is all.

Still hunting has many of the elements of trail watching or driving. In addition it has an arcane obligation all its own. Once you master the intricacies of still hunting, it is a very effective way of taking deer. But it imposes a discipline, personal and collective, which can never be ignored. It is, as you know, much more than a casual walking through the woods, hoping that a deer will get up within range of your rifle or bow. Demands will be made on every bit of your woodcraft. But once this method of taking deer is touched with your full knowledge of the game, it is a thrilling, effective way of taking a big trophy buck.

Chapter 18

Making a
Still Hunting
Drive

DRIVING deer is a misnomer, pure and simple. Deer are never driven. They are moved, but the direction in which they are moved is up to the game itself. An experienced deer hunter, conversant with deer habit, knows beyond the least shadow of doubt the probable direction the game will take when put up by drivers. The fact of two, three, or a dozen hunters making a cast through deer territory doesn't give direction to this game movement. So driving is a misnomer. We are stuck with the term, however, and it will be used as a term for this cooperative still-hunting drive, and subject to a very broad interpretation.

All through this *guide* emphasis has been placed on deer habit and their reaction to hunting. The points made previously have just as much application when you are making a drive as they do in still hunting, trail watching, or area watching. A properly conducted drive has all these elements in its makeup.

In still hunting, you move to conform to deer habit, using game trails, hunting in the direction of normal deer movement for the time of day, weather, season. In setting up a deer drive these factors must be remembered and applied.

Consider the reaction of deer to the orthodox noisy drive. When deer are put up by a group of hunters working a territory, they do one of two things: move out into other security cover or avoid the

150

drivers and remain directly in the cover which is being beat out. It is surprising the number of deer not moved across the stands by this noisy drive, a type of hunting effort which should be discarded as inefficient and unproductive.

In a previous chapter on still hunting, I reported my experience in working a bit of cover *after* such a noisy drive had taken place. It was no accident that the buck I put up and killed had remained in the territory all during the drive. The hunters themselves spelled out every move they made. More, they tried to push him across a stand he had no logical cause to use. Yet, he fell to a simple still-hunting plan of mine, one which conformed all along the line to game habit.

To get proper deer driving in perspective, let's review game requirements to which we must conform to be at all successful. This area must contain good security cover—a place where deer can shelter for the day against normal intrusion and storm. It should be within reasonable proximity of good feeding territory. It must have good escape coverage beyond its boundaries so that when deer *are* moved there is a logical way for them to go out toward other security cover. For you can never drive deer *away* from other security cover.

In working this bit of territory, drivers must comply with certain limiting factors of pace, noise, and, of course, direction. Broken down in detail these factors underscore the basic hunting techniques best used for a proper still-hunting drive.

Pace is probably the least understood of all successful driving. This basic essential can never be too slow for best results. It's still hunting all over again. The driver's moving snail-slow, pausing to scan the cover ahead, keeping to the logical pathways of the game.

Spacing of the drivers is very important for two reasons. First, of course, is proper coverage of an area. Second, is spacing in relation to the other drivers to keep the movement oriented, and most important in the direction of the individual stands. Assuming a typical piece of northern white tail cover, this spacing can well be 60 to 75 yards apart. At this interval in the line of drivers, they can occasionally see the hunters to either side. They can check the progress of the line and keep it fairly well in order. Deer trying to move around an individual driver are usually intercepted when this interval is kept. For lighter cover there can be wider spacing.

No loud noise, please. No, nothing save a cautious still hunting toward the posted hunters. Each hunter works toward the individual stand fronting him. But all during the drive he must remember that he is essentially a still hunter.

If the territory driven is properly selected, it is the very type favored for still hunting—open woods, bits of security cover, deer trails leading from each of the dense bit of brush where deer normally bed for the day. Deer, of course, are usually driven *after* their morning feeding period, and under stable weather conditions the thermal is giving them scent off their back trail.

Here, as you probably suspect, is the only difference between lone still hunting and a still-hunting drive. The still-hunting drive should be from the direction of the feeding area *toward* the security cover. *The driver moves with the thermal wind drift to his back.* When storms cancel out the normal wind drifts, new directions must be given to the drive.

When you examine the implications of this type driving, you can see that it has beautiful application. The game is never greatly alarmed. They feel they are familiar with the setup—master of it. They have bedded, or at least have moved to the dense clumps of huckleberry, hardhack, and hemlock thickets. Now, with the thermal bringing them news off their backtrails, they are all set, so to speak, for a casual day before moving out, nose-to-wind, to their feeding, *before* the thermal reversal.

A buck, so securely bedded, has his first intimation of danger when the wind drift off the backtrails carries hunter scent to him. He is immediately concerned but not greatly alarmed. His black nose assesses the warning. His huge ears are funneled forward to pick up any suggestion of hunter noise, and if he is a mature buck he has heard the usual loud hunter noise time after time. Now, however, he hears an occasional twig snap, spelling out the slow pace of an unalarmed deer. He hears the soft brush of hunting clothes against the low-growing cover, something with which he is very familiar because he has heard other deer make the same noise. This time, though, the addition of hunter scent to the familiar pattern is something else again.

Be sure, he isn't going to crash out of his security thicket at once. He'll wait around for the situation to develop. He'll watch those backtrails, assessing the possibility of staying where he is. His response to this type driving is entirely different than if the effort was one of those loud drives. Then, he would know with exactness the progress of *all* the drivers. Ten chances to one he would simply slip out of harm's way, let the drive go by, flushing the lesser deer, while he returned to his interrupted snoozing.

He *may* wait it out when you put on a still-hunting drive. But if he does, he has only *one* driver pinpointed, and that after he has moved in close. If he tried to slip around this driver, he is going to come in range of the other hunters. The shot can be taken safely *if* all the drivers know beyond the least uncertainty where each is at the time the deer presents himself. But when the driver fronting this particular cover does move in close, the cautious approach of the driver usually underscores another alternative he has: that escape trail leading away toward other security cover. He'll use this when the chips are down, sure as sure.

I can be positive of his usual reaction for the reason that I have been in at the kill of hundreds of true trophy bucks, finagled by this still-hunting drive technique. They are *all* educated to the possibilities of a noisy drive. But when a still-hunting drive is put on for their inspection, it injects an element of predation to which they have been conditioned for ages: moving on trail with the scent carried to the bedding game as warning, touching off their age-old instinct to use the escape trail when danger approaches the security cover.

Drivers, even with the wind at their backs, get many opportunities for shots. These shots are usually presented by deer moving on cross trails leading into the main escape pathways. Trails, even at the expense of reiteration, may show only casual markings. They may also be well cut up with tracks. In any event, they are always obvious enough to keep the drivers well oriented.

How about the stands occupied by hunters in a deer drive? Here is a fertile place for mistakes. I have seen deer stands, posted time after time, whose only merit is that they give a wonderful field of fire, if a deer should cross. This, alone, is their only inspiration, for there is no reason for a deer to ever approach them.

One very good example of this comes to mind. This posting covers about an acre opening. The cover beyond this is sparse, affording no chance for concealment. Yet, to my knowledge a hunter has covered this several times each autumn, for the past fifteen years. Not once has it produced. But, if a deer did cross here it would afford beautiful shooting.

153—Making a Still Hunting Drive

Essentially, a deer stand must comply with game habit, just as all other hunting complies. When deer are moved from the security cover after the early morning feeding period, their plans, outlined by the trails leading away from the cover, are quite obvious. They'll move out noses to wind. They'll move toward the next security cover. And the trails used will give the best wind coverage during the movement.

Under stable weather conditions trails used are different from those employed when it is stormy, even though the destination is the same in both cases. Postings, to be effective, must take full advantage of these changes. For example, one posting east of my cabin harbors the deer when there are stable weather conditions. This stand is made about two-thirds of the way upslope on a ridge. Deer moved from the acre patches of huckleberry brush below this, come out and upridge, nose-to-wind. But these same deer, sheltering in the same security cover, angle around the base of the ridge when the thermal or storm wind is upslope, then the posting is farther down ridge, with the hunter remaining *above* the cross trail.

Assess the dense cover behind the section you plan to drive. Make your postings in reference to the weather, at those points where the game can be intercepted to best advantage. The last consideration is field of fire, for it is patently obvious that you first must have something at which to shoot, if the stand is to be worth posting.

A hunter on stand has two obligations, primary and secondary. First of these is *safety*. This is the primary consideration on *all* stands. He must remember that the deer trails leading to his stand will be used by the drivers as well as the game. He must take up a position where there is no necessity of shooting back into the brush toward the drive. In short his stand must be covered in such manner that he is shooting across trail, away from the drivers *and* away from the other standers.

Remember, the deer moved by the drivers will escape nose-to-wind. This doesn't mean, of course, that *all* the trail has direct wind coverage. As they move out they will get news of any menace ahead of them. But there will be sections of trail which have cross currents, the wind given direction by the contour of the hills.

It is imperative that the hunter select a position below the trail or well to one side for his watching, a consideration secondary only to the safety angle. This posting should preclude all chance of putting hunter scent downtrail in the direction from which the deer will approach. A bit of study will indicate wind drift on the stand. A few powdered leaves dropped from shoulder height will spell out wind direction. So will smoke from a pipe or cigarette.

If you have an opportunity to conduct a pre-season studying of areas which you plan to drive, so much the better. When you are not under the compelling necessity of hunting, such study can be doubly productive in shaping up your drive after the season is open. You can work out the game trails. You can pinpoint the security cover, blaze a small cross on a tree to indicate a deer stand. This will not only make future hunting more productive, it is also a fascinating hobby in itself.

I have worked out such postings on several of my home-range hunting spots. In addition to studying the postings under all types of weather conditions, I have blazed pathways to these deer stands so a hunter can move unerringly to the posting without any chance of being misplaced or lost. The inspiration for blazing a pathway to the various stands came from the fact that on several occasions, hunters who were not taken to the stand, watched the wrong area just when a good-sized deer crossed the stand where he should have been.

Emphasis has been placed on cautious still hunting for the driver. This caution is equally important for all standers. Even in approaching the stand, there should be no loud crashing through the brush—still hunting. Time your drives with this in mind. Never hurry the standers to their postings, allow plenty of time for them to ease into position. You cannot relax the caution in any department required for a productive drive. The hunters who are taking up positions on stand should be cautioned about getting to their stations, quietly, slowly, and with the wind direction always in mind. *The game should have no intimation of hunter activity at any point, until the still-hunting drive begins to unfold. Under any circumstances it should never be aware of the posted hunters.*

Once a hunter is on stand, he must, above all, remain quiet. This, of course, starts with proper clothing, soft napped wool preferred—clothing having enough warmth so that there is no occasion for a hunter to stamp his feet or beat his arms about his body to restore circulation. Get into a comfortable position, one which can be maintained for an hour, two hours. Stay put. This is no small undertaking, any more so than it is in proper trail or area watching, but it is essential.

In the over-all consideration of driving deer, there is one factor which can trip you up more often than any. This is trying to cover too much territory, of trying to move deer too far. A drive should be reasonably short. It should be limited to a specific piece of cover, usually one section of good security area. Driving just one section of security cover makes for more efficient posting. For always, there is a link-up with adjoining security cover, and between these two sections there are always several trails which can be posted to advantage.

How many hunters for a successful still hunting drive? This has several right answers. The over-all consideration should be to keep your hunting parties small. A too large hunting party is hard to handle. Too much time is lost while waiting on the party to shape up for a drive. A party of five is almost ideal for the short productive drives, three hunters doing the still hunting toward the stands, with two hunters posted. In some sections this might be increased to eight hunters. Above this number the disadvantages far outweigh the advantages.

The smallest number, of course, is two hunters—one hunter posted, one hunter doing the still hunting. And this, of course, brings us directly back to still hunting itself—if it can be said that we have ever left it. For first, last, and all the time it is a basic consideration.

Chapter 19

When a
Deer Is
Wounded

Last autumn, during a morning's hunt, I put up a big four pointer in a tangle of huckleberry brush. He crossed in front of me and disappeared along a heavily brushed ridge. He wasn't moving fast, but the huckleberry brush only gave me intermittent flashes of those beautiful ivory tipped antlers and small sections of his glossy coat.

I could have shot on two occasions with very good chances of success. Both rifle and bullet were right for the occasion—a 6.5 X 55mm, handling a long, 160-grain, round-nose, soft-point bullet with a muzzle velocity of 2,400 feet a second. This bullet, surely, would have plowed through the intervening brush with top-drawer efficiency. Yet, there was a chance of wounding, so I let this buck go.

One doesn't, as a matter of course, gamble with a splendid trophy such as a deer. This is perhaps an arcane obligation about which an experienced deer hunter becomes increasingly aware over the seasons. He sees many dead deer which have been wounded and allowed to escape. Then, too, there is another consideration.

The kill is often the least important element of a successful hunt. When I worked my way still hunting to within 65 feet of this bedded buck, I had the best part of the hunt under my belt. This was emphasized when he came out of his bed in the huckleberry brush, those ivory tipped antlers agleam with the morning mist. Sure, I would have taken him if he had presented me with an opportunity for a clean kill. But any shot which might have wounded him would have canceled out my pride in the still hunting which put him under my rifle.

But despite the self-discipline which will prevent you from gambling on shots at half-obscured targets, there will be occasions when you'll wound deer. Your obligation for tracking and recovering this wounded game is just as exacting and personal as that of any of your hunting.

When a deer *is* wounded, there is a definite routine which you must follow if you are to recover it. A shot at any deer must always be carefully investigated, even though you are convinced that it is a clean miss. You must know all the signs of a hit, some of which are not in the least obvious. For example, a change of pace by the game is always a fair indication that it has been touched by a bullet. If your deer is moving at a walk when you fire and it breaks into a run, if it is running and speeds up at the shot, if it is standing and breaks into a run, all these spell a hit.

Usually, when an alerted deer is moving, it carries its tail high. If the tail is tucked in and lowered at the shot, this is evidence of a solid hit. If it is moving smoothly at any gait and at the shot the movement becomes labored or lacks rhythm, you have scored a hit. Quite often, however, a deer will take a hit without any indication of the occurrence. The exit trail should always be examined carefully after any shot. It is quite possible your quarry may be lying dead only a short distance beyond the point where you fired at it.

One autumn morning I trailed a deer across a series of logging slashes where there had been selective tree cutting. I expected to get a shot at any moment. The trail was smoking fresh, with the tracks wide, well set from a center line and showed drag marks—all of which encouraged me to stay with this particular trailing, regardless of the temptation to look in on some promising thickets. Suddenly, less than two hundred yards away, a shot crashed out against the silence. I knew that my careful trailing was probably canceled out by some lucky hunter. But I continued on with the tracks.

Eventually, I topped out on a ridge and saw a hunter standing about halfway upslope. He looked across the draw at the edge of an alder-fringed thicket. The tracks I followed turned in his direction, so I walked down to him. He had disappointment written all over him. "I never hope to get a better shot at a nicer buck," he said. "Browsing along the hill this side of that alder thicket, moving slow, and he never discovered me until I shot." He shook his head ruefully.

Range? About a hundred yards. Light? Excellent. The hunter was armed with a Model 94 Winchester Carbine .30/30, using a 170-grain bullet, a setup fully adequate for a clean kill. "Sure made him jump when I shot," the hunter observed. "He was in those alders in a flash. No chance for a second shot."

The action of this buck would have been a dead giveaway to a more experienced deer hunter. Hit he had been, beyond the least cavel of gunning doubt. I suggested that we examine the tracks, and the hunter followed me to the fringing alders. When we found where the buck had entered the heavy cover, the tracks showed uneven spacing. This buck had not run with a free stride. For the most part prints were well away from the centerline. But occasionally they were very close. This lack of rhythm in the buck's running showed that he was having trouble keeping on his feet. No blood sign was visible on the trail, but I did pick up a tuff of deer hair at the spot where the deer had been standing when the hunter shot.

We followed the track out for a short distance—a very easy task because the earth was plowed up by the buck's heavy running. Within twenty yards we found blood sign. Within thirty yards we found the buck, a beautiful five pointer, lying dead under a flame-colored maple, a heart shot, one which always proves fatal. Quite often, however, a deer receiving this fatal wound may move for as much as fifty or sixty yards before going down.

I left the hunter and his quarry and turned away through the reds and golds of the autumn forest. He was profuse with his thanks. More important, however, I doubt if he will ever take any apparent missed shot for granted. I think the episode took him out of the tyro class into the ranks of the experienced hunter, this beautiful buck he had lost *and found* marking the occasion.

The nature of the hit received is often indicated by the game itself. Trail sign complements this to a large extent and should be studied carefully. Blood on the trail tells a lot about the nature of the wound. Frothy, bright blood indicates a shot through the lungs. A deer taking this hit may run for some distance before going down. But when it is found it is invariably dead. A shoulder hit will not always anchor a deer, though, that is usually the case. Blood from this hit may be found well up on the bushes along the escape trail in heavy cover. In the more open forests it will be well to either side of the tracks. It also is brightly colored.

When a deer is paunched by the hunter placing his bullet too far back, the blood from the wound is very dark. The flow is not so great as from a hit in the shoulders, hips, or legs. A paunched deer may travel long distances, unless the trailing is done properly.

A front leg hit will usually show drag marks close to the centerline, with the three unwounded legs making normal impressions on the trail. When a hit is through the hams or one of the rear legs, the drag mark is equally obvious.

Before getting into actual trailing techniques, let's examine a few of the myths associated with wounded deer. Many hunters believe that a wounded deer will invariably run downhill. They further believe that any deer taking a hit will lower its tail. They feel that both these distress symptoms must occur to prove that a deer has been hit rather than missed. Sure, nearly all deer drop their flags when hit. But there are exceptions to this. As a plain matter of hunting fact, you'll often see deer sneaking out with the tail carried straight out behind, or tucked in close to the rump. As for wounded game running downhill, there are many exceptions, which we'll consider later.

Suppose you have wounded a deer, this fact established by a careful examination of the trail. From the blood sign you know that your deer has taken a hit too far back—paunched. What is to be done?

You have probably been told that you should wait two or three hours for your wounded deer to lie down and stiffen up. This routine is subject to a lot of qualifications. First and foremost is the time of day when you wounded your quarry. If the wounding occurred in the fore part of the day, wait for twenty or thirty minutes before beginning the tracking, provided the woods are not heavily hunted. If they are, you had best get on the trail at once before some other hunter puts his tag on your deer.

If the wounding occurs in mid-afternoon or later, you have only a limited time for tracking, and you had best get on the trail at once. Weather conditions also qualify the amount of time you should spend before taking up the tracking. Rain, sleet, or snow on the trail cancels out sign, especially blood sign, very rapidly. It doesn't make sense to wait around any length of time under these circumstances.

Beyond these considerations, there is the game's reaction ·to a hit. The shock of a hit is not painful. It tends to weaken the animal, so it instinctively seeks dense sheltering cover in which to lie down. If the wound is sufficiently severe and blood loss is great, the deer will seldom get to its feet again. Waiting for any great interval before taking up the trailing makes no contribution to recovering your game.

I usually work out the first 50 yards of trail at once, going cautiously, ready for a finishing shot. This length of trail usually established the nature of the wound and the probable dense cover toward which the wounded deer is traveling.

After studying the tracks on this initial run-out of trail, I take careful, accurate measurement of the tracks—length and width. In addition, I study the individual tracks for slight deviation from the norm. Hoofs chip and break under normal use. There will be wavy lines along the outer edge and splits and square breaks across the toes, making the track as individual as finger prints.

Once you have established the individual characteristics of these prints, you'll have no trouble in identifying the trail of your wounded deer, even if most of the sign is canceled out by the weather. For, always, there are sections of trail sufficiently protected from storm to hold well shaped up for several hours, individual tracks.

When you begin to go after your wounded deer, you should have a mass of information about it, including the nature of the wound. You must possess the ability to identify the individual tracks of your quarry, even if the trails have a maze of other tracks to confuse the issue. You'll have to demonstrate

Here is your rucksack, hunting knife, axe, and binoculars. The pack contains emergency rations, but the entire outfit need not weigh more than just a few pounds.

woodcraft of a high order, to be sure. But none of the requirements are beyond your good ability once you recognize the
problem in all its complexities.

Once, a party of us were out on a rainy afternoon, and one
man wounded a buck about twenty minutes before nightfall.
We had little time for tracking, so there was no waiting around.
We got on the trail at once. I say "we" advisedly, for only the
hunter who had done the shooting and myself took on the task
of recovering the game. By nightfall we had learned a lot about
that deer. The wound was high on the shoulder, indicated by
blood smear on the bushes after the game had slowed to a walk.
It was bleeding profusely, with the bullet ranging through,
with blood smear on both sides of the trail where it passed
through a small clump of dense growing huckleberry brush.

Despite the shoulder wound this deer had turned uphill, then
moved along just below the ridge for a short distance. Here we
had to abandon the trail because of darkness. I tied a white
handkerchief to a bush to mark the point. Before leaving the
tracking, I made accurate measurements of the prints. I noted
especially a square break across the left toe of the right hind
foot. That would be my identifying mark later.

When we abandoned the trail that night, with every intention
of returning and taking up the task of recovering the deer next
morning, I was certain I could identify the tracks of this deer
under any circumstances—just as you could have with the same
detailed evidence I had collected.

Next morning at good shooting light, the hunter who had
wounded the deer and I returned to our tracking. In the meantime the rain had washed out all blood sign of the previous
evening. Also, during the night, other deer had passed over the
trail, their tracks effectively canceling out what little sign might
have escaped the storm.

Standing at the segment of trail where I had tied the white
handkerchief, the prospect of finding the wounded deer didn't
appear good. But we did have several intangibles of deer habit
upon which to base our search. This we knew, in addition to
the nature of the wound and the ability to identify the tracks,
he would bed as quickly as possible in the nearest heavy cover.
Where wounded deer are trailed over long distances, the inspiration for this traveling is usually inept trailing by the hunter

who is attempting the recovery. I knew that he might go to cover uphill or down. But one thing was sure, he wouldn't travel farther than necessary to find the required thickets in which to hide.

With the weather canceling out sign as it had done, our best procedure was to hunt out the immediate heavy cover along the trail where the last sign had been established. This could be most effectively done by cooperative still-hunting-driving. The heaviest piece of cover, the one offering the greatest security was an acre patch of black huckleberry brush. The trail of the wounded buck stopped just short of this, with a well used trail continuing on into it.

My hunting partner moved around this island of huckleberry brush so he could command the trails leading out of it. These trails, incidentally, were three in number, as we discovered later. One angled along the easterly trend of the slope; another coursed downslope, holding to the face of the ridge; one looped over the ridge and led away to the north. All these, obviously were shaped by the varying wind drift over the season. Today, with the rain continuing, the watcher had to be well downslope to keep from tipping off any game in the thickets, because of the down draft channeled by the draws and creeks.

My partner, at my direction, angled around the huckleberry brush, downslope, and took up a position where he could watch any exit trail beyond the cover I planned to work out in detail.

Under one low sheltered bush, well protected from the rain, I found one of our buck's distinctive tracks and one tiny spot of blood. I moved in cautiously, following a deer trail, greatly reassured. At some points the brush was so thick I had to crawl. Half way through the thicket I placed my hand in our buck's empty bed. The blood smear left no doubt it was the right deer. A moment later I heard my partner fire. I waited. Then came a whistle on an empty cartridge case, our signal for a kill.

When I made my way on through the huckleberry brush, I found a very happy hunter examining a four pointer. This deer had been lightly wounded and would have recovered. The original wound was just above the backbone behind the shoulders. Had the bullet been two inches higher it would have been a clean miss. Yet, with this very light wound our quarry had taken to the heavy cover and layed up.

The essential factor of this recovery, it seems to me, was the very pertinent fact that we took nothing for granted from the very start of the tracking. We covered every possibility, just as if we were working that particular cover with unwounded game in mind.

Where two hunters are attempting to recover wounded game, the division of effort should be distinct. It is always better for one hunter to trail, the other to watch *and* do the shooting. Quite often as in this instance, the hunter doing the shooting will cover indicated trails. If the territory is fairly open, he'll be most effective just pacing the hunter doing the tracking—always alert for the shot, his eyes constantly on the cover ahead of the tracker.

The tracker unraveling the trail sets the pace. The watcher should never advance beyond the trail established by the tracker, nor should he put himself in a position where he cannot take the shot if the game is jumped. At times the tracker will lose the trail momentarily. Wait, watcher, keep your eyes on the cover ahead. Let the tracker cast about for the trail, which he will eventually re-establish. Quite often his efforts in casting about for the trail will jump the wounded game.

If you are hunting alone and wound a deer, then it is a problem of *still hunting and tracking,* where both the arcane obligations of watching and trailing must be assumed by you alone.

Trailing wounded deer on snow is much simpler than trailing on bare ground, but the technique is essentially the same. On snow, blood sign stands out sharply. Tracks are distinct, all of which is a big help in the recovery. Here, as in tracking wounded deer on bare ground, recovery is mostly a matter of methodical persistence.

Chapter 20

After
the
Kill

WHEN a big trophy buck falls before your rifle, the end product of your careful still hunting, or you have intercepted him while on stand, there is a glow of satisfaction in the occurrence which is hard to define. You'll feel, and rightly, that there is no hunting reward comparable to this. It is something you'll remember in exacting detail—just how the maples stood in their crimsons, golds, and autumn browns, the evergreens touched with a rim of frost—everything. But you are a long way from the kitchen with your kill, and many things can happen to that prime venison unless it is handled properly.

Venison, handled properly from kill to kitchen, is second to none in flavor and in tenderness. Recently I interviewed a butcher at a processing plant where local hunters take their deer to be cut and wrapped for deep freezing. My primary question was: "How many of these deer received for processing were actually fit for human consumption?" This butcher, who cuts and wraps as many as one hundred deer each autumn, didn't hesitate a moment in giving me an estimate. "Not over 40 per cent," he said. In short, sixty deer out of every hundred received couldn't be classed as actually fit for the table.

Much of this poorly handled venison can be traced directly to the myths and half-truths which are current about the proper manner of handling the kills. Basically, venison is no different in its handling requirements, including dressing out, than another meat, if the good flavor is to be preserved. Handled right, there is no strong racid "wild taste." But if good prime beef were given the same treatment which a lot of venison is given, it, too, would have a gamy flavor.

Here are some of the myths about handling venison which are accepted as gospel truth by many hunters. Venison should be allowed to season without the hide being removed. The deer should be bled immediately after the kill. The testicles of a buck should be removed at once to insure sweet meat. Venison always has a gamy flavor which must be disguised with a spicy sauce at the cooking. All these accepted ideas about venison are wrong.

Suppose we consider that buck lying dead before your rifle. Sure, it is natural that you would like to show him off to your neighboring hunters, but don't. Make some pictures of the occurrence. They'll be more enduring and will stand as a permanent record of the happening. The best recommendation of your deer hunting know-how will be how that prime venison tastes when you have your deer-hunting friends in for an after-season dinner.

Suppose this buck you downed is taken at the height of the rut. This, surely, as you have heard, is supposed to produce strong, gamy venison. But does it? No. Not if you go through the routine of dressing your game properly. Bleed him? After he has received a body hit with a high powered rifle? The bleeding has been well attended to, as you'll discover when you open the body cavity. You'll discover several of the major arteries and veins have been cut by the bullet and the body cavity is full of blood.

Your first step in insuring prime venison is to remove the *tarsal and metatarsal glands.* These, in spite of their strange sounding names, are easily located on the hind legs of the deer. They will vary in size on the Mule Deer, the Whitetail, and the Columbia Blacktail. But they are all equally adept in producing a very strong, disagreeable odor, a prime source of that "gamy" flavor so many venison recipes are supposed to hide.

The *tarsal glands* show as roughed sections of hair at the hock joints *inside* the hind legs. Cut around them and skin them out. Before throwing them away, I suggest that you smell of them to see how offensive this odor is. The *metatarsal glands* are on the *outside* of the hind legs about five inches below the hock joints. These, too, are easily located by the roughed appearance of the hair covering them. Cut well around them, skin them out and throw them away. After this, carefully clean your knife and hands with moss and fern to make sure none of this odor is transferred to the venison. Now you are ready to proceed with the routine of dressing out your buck.

First, cut from the brisket to the vent, just through the hide. This requires a sharp hunting knife for most efficient performance. When this cut is made, the hide will pull away from the incision, exposing the underlying tissue. Pull up a small amount of tissue in your left hand. Make a small slit with your knife. Insert two fingers of your free hand to serve as a guide and shield for the point of your knife blade. Press the body contents away from the knife as you open up the body cavity, following the original cut. Keep the knife blade well shielded *between* the first and second finger of your free hand so there will be no cutting of the intestines.

After this incision is made, cut around the penis, freeing it and the testicle sack as you work toward the vent. Just behind the testicles a piece of string is used to make two wraps around the penis. This is drawn up snug and tied. Now cut the penis and testicles off. Trace the remaining penis back toward the vent, freeing it by separating from the underlying tissue.

This operation will carry back to the vent. Cut around the vent, freeing it from all tissue in as far as you can reach with your knife, being careful not to puncture the lower intestine. Pull this out a bit and tie another piece of string around the vent so there is no chance for the contents to escape.

Make sure that the penis is freed of its surrounding tissue at this point. Now, with these operations completed, you can reach through the body incision and pull the large intestine and penis through, and out the body cavity. Tilt your deer on its side and the rest of the intestine and paunch will fall out.

This procedure will expose the diaphragm just forward of the paunch. Cut through the diaphragm carefully, following the outline of the rib cage, making the first cut from the brisket to the backbone on one side only. Reach up forward through this cut, beyond the heart and lungs, and cut the windpipe. Grasp the windpipe and pull down smartly. This will free the lungs and heart. Cut the attachment at the backbone, near the shoulders. Trace out the rest of the diaphragm with your knife and all the body contents may be emptied out.

Now is a good time to cut the heart and liver free. Lay these aside on some clean leaves or moss, after wiping them free of blood. A plastic bag is a good container in which to bring them out of the woods. Once out of the woods they should be washed of all blood, then put to soak in slightly salted water, the water being changed as often as it discolors with blood.

When the body contents are removed, you'll notice that the body cavity is well filled with clotted blood, the results of your shot, and a prime indication that cutting a deer's throat to bleed it after the kill serves little purpose. The blood in the body cavity must be removed at once. To do this, turn your deer's head uphill. Roll the body over so the body cavity is toward the ground. If there is no snow on the ground, see that there are clean leaves or moss beneath the kill during this routine. Now pick your quarry up slightly, grasping it by the antlers and getting the chest section high enough so that any blood will drain out. If you have a hunting partner to help you with this, so much the better. A lot of clotted blood will run out during this operation. You can now turn your deer over and proceed to wipe the body cavity clean of its remaining blood, using moss or a handful of leaves for this purpose.

You may be tempted to use water for this cleanup. Don't, not even a dampened rag, though a dry rag is excellent. If you attend to this with moss or leaves, while the body is still warm, you can do a very acceptable job, with no chance of the meat souring.

At this point you are confronted with two alternatives. You can carry your deer out to a more convenient place before removing the hide, or you can, if you are properly equipped, remove the hide at this point. If you decide to take your deer out with the hide on, you may drag it, if there is snow on the ground to cushion the operation. If you are hunting on bare ground, dragging is to be avoided as it bruises the meat. Two hunters can carry it on a pole—a very awkward operation. Or, if the deer isn't too large and heavy, it can be made into a backpack.

This is done in the following manner. First, skin out the legs from the hoofs, retaining the dew claws on the hide. Near the knee and hock joint you'll find a place where the skinned out portion of the leg is easily severed. When this is done on all four legs the right front leg and left hind leg are tied snugly together using the skinned out hide. Repeat this operation with the left front leg and right hind leg. Those dew claws will prevent the two knots from slipping. Now you have a woodsman's pack. You can slip your arms through the tied legs, settling the skinned out portions across your shoulders.

If you are carrying your deer out in this manner in heavily hunted territory, it is always best as a safety measure to cover it with a piece of scarlet cloth, or a scarlet hunting jacket.

Once out of the woods and to your hunting camp or lodge, skin your game at once. Then cover it with a game sack. The sooner the hide is off the better from the standpoint of prime venison. Sure, unskinned buck looks nice on a game pole, but after a deer drops before your rifle, your primary concern is with bringing out good tasty venison.

The other alternative to bringing your deer out with the hide on it is to skin it at the spot where you field dressed it. This is much to be preferred, if you are prepared to handle it properly. In another chapter hunting rucksacks will be considered. Here, it is sufficient to indicate their necessity if you are to bring your deer out of the woods fully dressed, quartered, and ready for the aging. Indeed, this aging starts immediately at the dressing. So, properly done, there is much to be said for woods dressing your deer from start to finish.

You'll have to hang your deer for the skinning, and for this particular routine there is nothing better than those light-weight blocks or stretchers advertised in most sporting magazines. These are rigged with nylon lines and are capable of picking up the largest deer. In addition to these blocks you should have two small sections of nylon cord testing around 500 pounds. These should be tied to form two loops about fourteen inches long when stretched between your hands. One of these is half-hitched around the antlers of your deer, or around the neck, if you have killed a doe. The other loop is half-hitched over a limb to receive one end of the block used for hoisting. With this setup there is no great difficulty in swinging a deer free of the ground.

Please note that the deer is hung by the head for skinning. This is important, for you can take the hide off without the hair contacting the venison with the game hung in this manner.

Cut around the neck just below the ears to start your skinning, unless you plan on a head mount. In this case make a cut around the neck at the shoulders and brisket. Then another cut is made from the shoulder to the back of the head, along the neck. Skin this section out, starting at the head. Work the hide off the head with the ears attached. Careful skinning must be done about the eyes and nose to bring the hide off with the black nose attached, the eye slits undamaged. Salt this section of the skin lightly when you are in camp. Roll it flesh side to flesh side, and it will keep until you turn it over to a taxidermist for mounting, along with the cleaned head, and the antlers.

Getting the rest of the hide off is comparatively simple. Make an incision on the inside of each front leg, connecting these up and across the brisket. Follow this by a cut from the intersection at brisket to the original cut around the neck, when the cape is not saved. Start at the head and skin downward. Take care that none of the hair side of the skin touches the flesh. The previously mentioned gland odors are very apparent in the hair of deer, so skinning must be done carefully to avoid contamination. These odors in the hair is another very good reason why the hide should be removed as soon as possible after the kill.

In skinning out, the hide can be "knuckled" off by pulling it out directly from the body, then pressing downward with your free hand at the junction of hide and flesh. Start the hide around the end of the front legs, then strip it toward the shoulder. The hind legs are "knuckled" free of the hide without splitting, the hide coming off "cased," or turning inside out as it is removed.

You'll notice that when you are skinning out your game at the scene of the kill, there is a vapor rising from the still warm meat. This is all to the good, and shows that it is properly curing. When the hide is left on until the meat is cold, this moisture is not allowed to escape, and it makes no contribution to the delicate flavor of properly cared for venison.

After the hide is removed, you have the problem of getting the meat out cleanly. For this operation a small hand-axe, such as you should always carry in your hunting rucksack, is used to split the deer down at the backbone. Do not attempt to split the backbone itself, but rather follow along one side of it at the point where the ribs are attached.

Free a front quarter down to the small of the back. Do the same at the brisket. Cut this quarter free. Have two clean sacks ready to receive the meat. These may be made up of white cloth for the purpose, but they can also be procured from a bakery where flour is brought in hundred pound sacks. It's best to only put one quarter to a sack, if two hunters plan on taking out the deer, for in this manner each quarter can be insulated from the other, without the warm meat coming in contact. One hunter is under the compelling necessity of making two trips in order to bring out his kill.

If at all possible, cache the hide, cape and antlers and recover them after the venison is taken out of the woods.

Once you have arrived in camp, the quarters should be hung for cooling, each separated and a large game bag placed over them to keep the meat away from flies. It should be thoroughly chilled before any attempt is made to take it home.

If you plan on staying in camp for some time after the kill, the quartered venison will keep perfectly and cure out well if it is hung in the shade.

Transportation is not much of a problem where the kill has been skinned properly and quartered. If the distance entails a stop-over, the quarters should be hung for the night in a cool place. Keep the meat away from car fumes. Best place to carry it is either on a trailer under a tarp, or carefully wrapped and placed in the car trunk.

The final endorsement of your careful handling from kill to kitchen is the venison on the table. Even at the expense of reiteration, anytime venison must be served with a heavy, spicy sauce to disguise its flavor, you can be sure that it wasn't handled properly at some stage.

Cutting and wrapping for your deep freeze is best done at the freezer-locker plant, where you have taken it for its final curing. If you *do* attempt the cutting, just remember that your venison should be handled the same as a prime baby beef or veal. Pamphlets on this phase of the routine may be had from the Department of Agriculture, Washington, D. C., or from your state Game Commission.

One last question, how long should venison be hung and seasoned before cutting and using? I place this at eight to ten days, when the hide has been removed at, or close to, the time of the kill. When the hide is left on for any appreciable length of time, it doesn't matter, for in spite of all you might do, you'll have venison with "gamy" flavor. This curing period, of course, includes the time the venison has been hung in camp. Best, of course, is immediate cooling in the special room assigned for this at the processing plant. If your hunt is close enough that you can immediately take your kill to the cooling room, the larger share of your prime venison problem is solved.

Chapter 21

Outfitting

for the Hunt

A deer hunter should never leave camp unless he is properly equipped for survival in an emergency, such as being lost in a storm or just plain being lost.

This, as you probably know, means meticulous attention to equipment other than a rifle, shotgun or bow and arrow. Foremost among requirements is a *hunting rucksack*. This particular bit of equipment serves a multitude of outdoor purposes. In it is carried the extra equipment needed for a deer hunt. It can be the means of bringing out the kill. Quite often, let it be whispered, its contents enables you to spend a not too uncomfortable night in the wilderness, if you are caught short by a storm, or if you become lost.

In a previous chapter on handling venison after the kill, I touched upon the rucksack as a means of getting the quartered meat to camp. This is a primary use. But beyond this requirement a properly selected rucksack is actually a piece of wearing apparel rather than a pack you carry.

A hunting rucksack need not be large, with the idea of holding a half deer. Actually, those quartered pieces of venison are *tied on the sack,* with the load serving as its own packboard. With a little experience and experimenting, you can easily achieve this. All that is required are several D rings attached securely to the

174

rucksack along the sides, at the bottom and top. Nylon cord is used to lash the load together, the hind quarter of venison turned and located so that the meat cushions the pack next to your back and shoulders, when you get into the carrying straps.

Your extra sweater, jacket or plastic tarp which you carry in your rucksack as a matter of course, can also be arranged within the pack for additional cushioning.

See that the bottom of the carrying straps are firmly secured to the bottom of the meat burden. See that the top of these straps are also secured near the top of the meat sack, all this achieved with a length of nylon cord. I carry about fifteen feet of such cord for this purpose. It also serves in making an overnight plastic tarp windbreak, to anchor tree boughs, and sometimes for a clothes line to dry equipment before the campfire.

A hunting rucksack should have broad shoulder straps. In addition, it should come equipped with a belt. This belt serves two purposes. It takes a bit of the weight from the shoulders while hunting. Also it keeps the bag close to the body, a very essential item when you are moving about in brush.

A rucksack of the nature described may be had from several suppliers. But most of them lack a waist band. This you can attach, procuring a length of canvas belting from any store dealing in War Surplus. Some rucksacks, designed for mountain climbing, come with a suitable waistband. It is a matter of shopping around until you find a rucksack which is not too wide, hangs well from the shoulders and is provided, or can be provided, with a waistband.

I have two leather straps and buckles attached to the top flap of the sack. This I use to carry an extra sweater or hunting jacket. Sometimes, I carry rain clothes here, rolled in a scarlet cloth. Your rucksack, it goes without saying, should be waterproof, usually of light reinforced canvas.

What should be in this rucksack while you are prowling the wilderness hunting deer? First item is a waterproof match box. This, full of matches, is a reserve and should be carried in addition to your usual supply, if you smoke. A second item is a hand-axe, such as Marbles, with either a leather guard or blade protector. Such an axe weighs but little. Yet, it is your most essential piece of equipment other than your rifle. It can be used for dressing out game. It may mean the difference between survival and disaster. With matches to build a fire, and this axe to cut fuel and prepare a windbreak, you can survive any type of weather.

The third item associated with your hunting rucksack should be a hunting knife. This should normally be carried *in* a special pocket of the pack, along with the previously mentioned hand-axe *and* a sharpening stone.

You can, of course, carry this hunting knife at your belt. But it is much better protected in the rucksack. A pocket knife can be carried in your trouser or hunting jacket pocket for incidental use, such as cutting twigs out of your way on a deer stand, or any other camp chore where a knife is required. Your hunting knife should be reserved for the task of dressing out your deer—this and nothing more, unless there is an emergency where it might serve better than your sturdy pocket knife.

This hunting knife, being a specialized tool, should be selected carefully. Avoid those five- and six-inch blade sheath knives. One of these may look impressive at your belt, but they are something less than effective in dressing out game A blade length of three and one half inches, to not more than four inches is best. It should be of such quality steel that it will hold a keen edge.

Other items carried in the hunting rucksack should be two or three squares of aluminum foil. These should each be about a foot square. They can be used for cooking over a bed of coals, serving as frying pans or stew pans. They weigh practically nothing and take up little space. Sometimes, if you happen to be caught short and must stay out overnight, these can be used to cook any small game you manage to come by, such as a rabbit, grouse, or squirrel to supplement your emergency rations.

In addition, I carry a quart can with a bail and wire hook to hang over a fire. Inside this I have several bags of tea, a quarter-pound of sugar, a folding cup. Here, again, the weight is scarcely felt.

A quarter-pound of pancake mix *and* a half-pound of bacon. Three or four chocolate bars and a half-pound of rice is carried. All this is logical for wilderness hunting in such places as sections of the west, Michigan, Maine, and Canada.

The entire contents of your hunting rucksack, including these emergency rations, should never weigh more than five or six pounds—really nothing when the weight is caught up at the shoulders and waist, as it should be with a well fitted rucksack.

This is a basic list I have suggested. It has served me well, so much so, that in solitary hunting, if the exigency of the situation demands it, I often make an overnight camp, resuming my hunt on the morrow, with the previous day's activity shaping it up to a great extent. Again, if a storm forces you to shelter, first make camp, then these rations alone, or supplemented by a rabbit or other small game, will see you through nicely, just as they have seen me through on occasion. Knowing that you are prepared for the worst the wilderness can dish out, gives you a free-wheeling confidence which makes hunting a pleasure.

You'll naturally carry a lunch, usually sandwiches, in addition to these basic items. But I am betting that if you carry the recommended quart can and tea, eventually you'll make a fire at noon and have tea, piping hot for the occasion. Most professional woodsmen, including myself, "boil the pot" at noon, with tea preferred as the drink.

One item of hunting equipment, while not usually carried in the hunting rucksack, should be given attention here. This is binoculars. Here, unless you understand the basic elements of optics, you can go wrong. Just remember that your binoculars must have plenty of light gathering ability, an exit pupil which complements the human eye.

The normal eye widens to about 5mm of light during late evening and early morning. Under very bright daylight, it adjusts to about 2.5mm. The light gathering ability of binoculars is indicated by dividing the power into the objective lens size. This indicates that those small binoculars of 6 power, with 15mm objective lens are no bargains. Dividing the 15mm objectives by the power (6), you come up with an exit pupil of 2.5mm, just enough light for good viewing under optimum light conditions. During early morning or late evening, these small palm-sized glasses are practically useless.

My choice, from the standpoint of portability and light gathering ability, is the Bushnell Broadfield. These light portable binoculars have a power of 6, with 25mm objectives. This combination gives an exit pupil of close to 5mm, and serves very well in dim woods, late evening or early morning. If there is enough light for shooting, there is plenty of light for effective use of these binoculars.

They have a wide, 600 foot field of view at a thousand yards and will prove very effective when examining logging slashes, fire scalds, and other wide open spaces. This wide field of view serves very well for close range work in heavy cover, too.

Best place to wear your binoculars is on a strap about your neck, if the glasses are light, such as these recommended ones. Heavy glasses, so worn, can prove very tiring during a day's hunt. The strap should be shortened enough so that there is no great tendency to swing as you stoop to pass under a low limb. Actually, you can dispense with the binocular case in most instances, and during rough weather, simply drop the binoculars in a front pocket of your shooting jacket, the binocular strap about your neck. Then, when you want them for viewing, they are immediately available. On occasion they will ride out a very severe storm, when they will not be used, in your hunting jacket pocket.

Just as essential as this listed equipment is the proper selection of hunting clothes. This clothing must serve two primary purposes: keep you comfortable during the hunt and protect you from other hunters who might mistake you for a deer. My thought, well weathered by several decades of deer hunting, is that there is nothing quite so good as wool for outdoor clothing. Sure, there are several insulated garments which do a boss job of keeping you comfortable, if you are not too active. But when you are moving one moment and inactive the next, I doubt if you find anything quite so efficient as wool in keeping you comfortably warm under all circumstances. Wool outer clothing and wool underwear or a wool-cotton combination if you cannot stand wool next to your skin.

An extra jacket carried to be slipped on when you are inactive is a must. The solution to this problem, which ties in directly with a hunting rucksack, is to have an extra coat or jacket into which you can slip while waiting. This, if put on immediately after you are on stand, before there is any chance to lose much body heat, will keep you warm all during the long wait. Take it off and replace it in your rucksack while driving for other hunters, or still hunting.

All deer hunting clothing should be soft napped, so there is no harsh brushing of coat or trousers on the cover. Here, as in all phases of deer hunting, you must achieve the same type noise as that of your quarry. A deer brushing against a bush produces the same soft sigh as proper hunting clothes brushing against it. This, as you know, is much less alarming than any noise readily identi-

178

fied as hunter made. This, too, spells out the necessity of using woolen clothing; and make it scarlet for color or a bright yellow in the interest of hunting safety. A wool cap is also a very good thought. But, if you are hunting in fairly damp woods, a bright red woolen hat with a fairly wide brim is best. It will keep your neck dry and prevent wet leaves from falling down beneath your collar.

Wool gloves will also pay their way. But in making ready for a shot, time can be consumed in removing one. Best is to carry a small handwarmer for your trigger hand. This warmer, placed in a side pocket of your hunting jacket, is easily reached by your trigger hand. Then when your bare hand becomes cold, it can be thrust into the pocket for a few moments. Some hunters wearing gloves, however, become very adept at grasping the glove on the trigger hand with the teeth, snatching it off immediatly for the shot.

Shoes for hunting should be equipped with soft, crepe rubber soles. These not only are good for keeping your footing, but they also achieve a very acceptable grade of hunter noise—the type the deer themselves make.

In wet snow, swampy ground, or rain there is no substitute for rubber. I usually take both types to hunting camp and am prepared for the exigency of hunting under all conditions. Socks should be of wool, and it is better to wear two medium weight ones, rather than a heavy pair. Feet are prone to swell on hunting trips if you are not used to hiking. With two pair of medium-weight wool socks, one pair can be removed to correct shoe fit.

You should give considerable thought to the size of your deer hunting boots and shoes. Cold feet are often a matter of poor circulation brought about by too tight footwear. A loose fitting boot or shoe is best, usually about one size larger than your street shoes. In buying and fitting, test with the two pair of medium-weight socks you plan to wear. Stand up, place your full weight on the shoes. If they feel loose and comfortable, they are of a proper size. If there is any suggestion of snugness, they will prove to be too tight for hunting.

Shoes and boots should be broken in thoroughly by pre-hunting season hiking. This hiking can be done on city streets, in parks, any place where you can walk a few miles on several occasions, testing and trying your footwear. As you break in your leather hunting boots or shoes, give them several applications of Neatfoot Oil. When they feel as comfortable as well used house slippers, you have them readied for your deer hunting.

One other piece of equipment you'll find essential, I have reserved for the last, a compass. You must know a practical way of using it under actual woods ranging conditions. This is so essential, I'll take the next, and last, chapter in touching upon selection and use.

Chapter 22

Woods Ranging
and the Problem
of "Lost Hunters"

To KEEP oriented at all times, a deer hunter must not only know the directions of his travels, but the distances as well. This is basic. The factor of distance is an imponderable which has tripped up more hunters than misdirection with which it is closely associated.

Deer hunters may speak of so many miles traveled in a day's hunting. Estimates will vary to a great extent, depending on the type of country hunted. Mileage is an inaccurate method of measuring wilderness distances. One of those superb woodsmen of the past, the North American Indian, would have abandoned it as useless had he known about it. Not even a surveyor can estimate distances accurately in rough country, reducing it to miles, yards, feet. In order to be accurate in *his* measurements, he must set up his compass, take exact sightings, then measure the ground by "chaining" it.

Obviously, if a trained civil engineer must go to all this trouble to measure distances accurately, no casual estimation by a deer hunter can even remotely approach accuracy of the distances he travels. How, then, is a hunter to know his distance from camp as well as the compass direction? *He must take a page from the Indian's book of woodcraft and measure all distances traveled in terms of time.*

Suppose you and I start from camp early one autumn morning. We have deer hunting in mind, even know in a general manner the wilderness where we'll hunt. Still, those broken hills, brushy beyond the telling, emphasize the necessity of always keeping direction, recording the distance traveled on each leg of our hunt.

Starting early, we travel in an easterly direction for three hours. In trending east, we do not keep an exact course on an east and west line. Our hunt swings north and south of this base line. We pause frequently in our cooperative still hunting. These pauses are only noted when they extend to more than five minutes. When they lengthen beyond this, such as the time used in glassing a fire scald for the better part of a half-hour—the time taken out for lunch and to boil the teapot, the intervals are deducted from our time spent moving.

If you were to pencil in our hunting route of the morning, using your note pad, the pattern of our movement would show a snake-like trace, but the direction would be east.

How far is camp? We started when there was still a handful of stars in the western sky. You looked at your watch. It read 6:30 a.m. When the questions occur about distance to camp, you again look at your watch. It is well along toward noon. Deducting the previously noted pauses, we have been on trail three hours. Our camp is three hours west. How many miles? Disregard the miles entirely. No wilderness trapper or Indian would translate travel time into miles. There is no particular reason for him to do so. We could easily turn and walk west to our camp, arriving well within the time limits indicated in our outward journeying.

We decide to hunt north. Here, at this drastic turning we carefully check our compasses, just as we have done every ten or fifteen minutes during the outward traveling. We also check the exact time when we changed our basic direction. This is important. After three hours travel east, we turn north. Trending north we meander west and east, but always our hunt is essentially north. Eventually we consume two hours on this leg of our day's hunt. Now we begin to think of returning to camp. By our back trail, if we wanted to follow it, we would have to cover five hours of distance—wilderness distance. Draw the first base line three hours, on your note pad, or in the mud of a deer trail. Add the north leg of the journey, two hours.

Now with the two legs of our hunt outlined, we draw a third

line connecting these two. It takes only seventh-grade math to see that our camp lies four hours of travel time southwest.

The readings during a day's deer hunt have been sufficiently accurate to pinpoint camp at any time, both as to direction and as to distance measured in time.

The essential requirement in using this method of keeping directions oriented is to select landmarks about your camp conspicuous enough to compensate for reasonable errors of travel. An oddly contoured hill set with differently shaped trees, such as maples in an evergreen forest, an open lake, a wide loop of stream —anything easily seen and identified when you are within a half hour or an hour of your camp.

Sometimes these landmarks complement each other. I have hunted a wilderness where the first landmark in reference to my camp was a segment of valley with a long exposed ridge behind it. Coming to this, I had a view of a bleached silver-weathered snag standing starkly alone at the top of a small rock butt. Beyond this, a half hour travel through a dense stand of red alder, I came to my small camp. First I had only to hit this section of valley, a very broad target, usually south of my hunting. Then, as I approached camp, the target narrowed until it indicated the end of my journeying for the day.

While I have touched upon only a few angles of the measurement of distance by using time as the basic yardstick, these are sufficient to always keep your hunt well oriented. The essential thing is to make sure of the time tie-in with any change of compass direction.

In using a compass there are many things to be learned and many more to be unlearned. There are maps of many wilderness localities showing the "variation" between geographic and magnet north. But a hunter, with the comparatively simple problem of keeping oriented during a day's hike, had best forget any thought of compass variation. Take a direct reading. Another term as essentially confusing is "deviation." This should not be confused with compass variation, even though each condition does influence the reading of a compass. Deviation of a compass needle is caused by the nearness of a mass of ferreous metal. Large natural deposits of iron ore will cause inaccurate readings—deviation. Even the hunting equipment you carry, such as rifle and axe may cause some deviation.

You may be advised to remove all your hunting equipment and go at least twenty feet away from it before taking a compass reading, a very impractical procedure. Actually, your only concession to the possible influence of your equipment on compass readings is to always keep your equipment and compass in the *same* relative positions for *all* readings. When this is done, you have consistent readings, sufficiently accurate to keep direction for a day's travel. I usually sling my rifle on my left shoulder while taking compass readings. I make sure that this relation of rifle and compass is maintained for all checking of directions.

Your best aid in remembering basic turning of your hunting directions, if you are prone to forget, is a small notebook and pencil. Jot down the trend of the hunt. Put down the time consumed. Note any basic change of direction. This sketch, added to during the day, keeps you informed of the hunt's progress at any time.

Topographical maps are invaluable aids to you in your wilderness hunting, but you need to have no slavish dependence on them. These maps show elevations marked in feet and are contoured at regular intervals. They also show all established roads and trail and water courses. Study such a map of the area you plan to hunt. Pinpoint your camp, but always measure the distances you travel in time consumed on the trail. Pencil this information in as you hunt. Eventually you'll have a very detailed map of the area.

One more requirement should be given your consideration before going into strange wilderness country. Use your compass in woods or open country which are totally familiar to you. Measure your travel time between two landmarks. Note the compass base line. Work out the problem of returning to your starting point without the necessity of backtracking. This can be done in a city park or a piece of open countryside, and it is very good training for wilderness ranging.

Before considering the selection of a compass for your deer hunting use, let's consider the problem of being lost, or of having one of your hunting party lost. In a previous chapter of this *guide,* consideration was given the selection of a hunting rucksack and emergency rations. This, of course, ties in directly with lost hunters, and compass use, too.

The basic factor to remember about being lost, and one which takes the panic out of the experience, is the knowledge that it occurred within a day's travel of camp, usually less. What places distance between camp and lost hunters is misdirected wanderings *after* becoming confused. Yet, if there is snow on the ground, the backtrail of such a lost hunter can be followed. It will lead to familiar ground within a very short period; or if followed long enough, directly into camp. This course is to be recommended if the hunter is out alone. It is not always the best procedure if he becomes lost from a hunting party.

Suppose you are of a hunting party who plans on hunting a section of Maine wilderness, a wilderness in the west, or any of the several states having large forested areas. It doesn't make good survival sense to start the hunt without the party agreeing in detail on procedures to be followed if one of the party becomes lost. First rule agreed upon is for the lost hunter to remain put. He should remember that he is within a very few short hours of camp. If he does wander, ten chances to one he'll make the problem of being found more complicated. But if he stops the moment he realizes he is unsure of directions, builds a fire, then shelters from the weather with a brush windbreak or plastic tarp, there is no great complication, even if he isn't found until the next day.

He has, or should have, emergency rations for two or three days. He has the means of building a shelter and making a fire. It is suggested, however, that he go through this routine a time or two before being under the compelling necessity of doing so while lost. In this manner he gets the feel of building a proper temporary camp—even cooking a meal.

Survival assets, while lost for any appreciable length of time, includes a hunter's ability to take small game with his rifle, such as a rabbit or ruffed grouse. His rifle also is used for answering signals. But it shouldn't be employed for this purpose until contact is made by the searching party by hearing their *signals*. Unless this procedure is followed, the lost hunter can dissipate his ammunition supply to no good purpose.

It should be thoroughly agreed upon by all members of the hunting party that when a member *is* missing for any length of time after a drive, a still hunting session or trail watching, three shots should be fired by one of the hunting party. The lost hunter hearing these, should respond with one shot. Thus contact is made.

If you are the lost hunter, take a direct compass reading on the sound of those three shots. If you are a member of the search party, take a direct compass reading on the one shot fired by the lost hunter. The searching party moves in the direction indicated until they need another confirming signal. Fire one shot. This should be answered immediately by the hunter who is lost. Sometimes, as the interval is closed, it will be necessary to exchange signals several times. Eventually you'll arrive at the position of the lost hunter to find the rascal thoroughly comfortable, a pot of hot tea on the fire and the entire experience something about which to laugh in camp.

The simplicity of this routine endorses its utilization. Make sure all members of the hunting party understand what they are to do under all circumstances—whether lost or a member of the searching party. Make sure, as a matter of plain hunting fact, that all members carry sufficient equipment for survival—especially matches and a small hand-axe.

If you are hunting alone and become confused as to directions, the problem is slightly different in that you must make your way out. You should never, however, enter any wilderness area without someone knowing where you are going, the time you plan to spend in the area, and the probable time of your return. Then, if you do become lost, help will eventually reach you. Hunting alone, though, you do have to try to make your way back to camp, a relatively simple problem.

You may, as previously indicated, backtrack in snow. You can, without any great effort, if you have kept a record of the time spent on trail and the general direction, pinpoint familiar territory in very short order. Best, when you do become confused, try to get back into familiar territory rather than reach directly for camp. Once in a section you recognize, the tie-in with camp comes as a matter of course.

Sometimes, you may be out for two or three days in a large wilderness. Yet, the episode has no problem over which you need worry, if you utilize all your resources provided by a proper rucksack, equipment, and a knowledge of wilderness ranging. Just remember that you are lost within a comparatively short distance of familiar territory. Work out the problem with this in mind. Never, if you are trying to orient yourself in reference to your starting point, attempt to travel in any direction unless you have good logical reasons to believe it will bring you to familiar territory or camp.

Draw a map of your backtrail, using the notes you have prepared in taking compass readings, measuring the distances traveled. Make this up to the point where you became confused. Remember all the basic turnings. Ten chances to one, when you have this data before you, the problem of getting on the beam again will prove relatively simple.

If you must stay out over night, allow the last two hours of daylight for building a shelter and the gathering of fuel for an all-night fire. Don't, under any circumstances, attempt to travel at night.

In a densely populated state, such as Pennsylvania, you can find your way out of the woodlands by finding a stream and following it downstream. Sooner or later it will bring you out to a town or a camp. Once out, you must get someone to drive you back to your camp and end the anxiety and work of the camp members searching for you.

In selecting a compass for your deer hunting, wilderness ranging, make sure you have one which is easily read. This simple requirement is not met by a number of instruments presently available. The greatest failure is a poorly marked needle. Sure, most of these are marked with a positive north end in white, red, or some other color, but quite often hunters are not sure in use which is north and which is the south end of the needle. The north end should be marked with a large N. Better yet is a needle shaped like an arrow.

Basic directions, north, east, south, west, and the degrees in between should be easily read under poor light conditions. It is needless to say that in addition to these provisions, a compass should be sturdy and capable of taking a reasonable amount of abuse.

Above all, learn how to use your compass before depending on it in a wilderness.

One very good compass which I have used for several years is the Leupold Sportsman. Another I can recommend is the Lensatic, manufactured by the Superior Magneto Corporation. This latter has a floating dial, with the entire compass card turning. It is well marked. In addition it carries "sighting lines" for taking a compass reading, as does the Leupold.

The wilderness in which you'll hunt deer is a fascinating and friendly place, but it places no premium on going unprepared in any department. Storms can come growling over the cover you hunt, dropping temperatures, obscuring landmarks and making travel difficult or impossible. The breed of men who can face up to these changing wilderness moods with confidence are those who go prepared for the worst. To them the experience is always richly rewarding. Storm or shine, it is always good hunting.

A map can tell you a lot about the country in which you hunt deer, but it must be related to your primary concern of keeping oriented with your camp.

Index